Colour and pattern in the home

Jill Blake

a Design Centre book
published by Quick Fox

Colour and pattern in the home
First edition published 1978
A Design Centre book published
in the United Kingdom by
Design Council 28 Haymarket
London SW1Y 4SU

Designed by Anne Fisher
Printed and bound in
the United Kingdom by
Jolly & Barber Ltd, Rugby

Distributed throughout the continents
of North America, including Canada,
and South America by Quick Fox,
33 West 60th Street, New York,
NY 10023

International Standard Book Number 0–8256–3137–8
Library of Congress Catalog Card Number 78–58485
© Jill Blake 1978

Contents

3

Introduction

This book is really about interior decoration. To many people the word 'decoration' means bringing out the stepladder and tools, preparing ceilings, walls and woodwork, then getting down to the somewhat tedious task of painting and paperhanging. This is why this book is called *Colour and Pattern in the Home*, because it will help you to choose these elements and to contrast textures to create a more attractive home, and one in which I hope you, and your family, will enjoy living.

Before you begin to decorate and furnish, you have to select and buy the various materials: wallcoverings, paint, floorcoverings, fabrics and so on; some people enjoy doing this, but others find it a bore. Whichever category you come into, I hope this book will help you to get a lot more fun out of homemaking, for this is the moment (before you buy a single pot of paint or roll of wallpaper) to look at your property with fresh eyes. Look to see if you are making the most of the space available – you could perhaps replan certain areas to do double-duty; change the function of some rooms; make some structural alterations and generally re-think the way in which you are living in the protective shell of bricks and mortar we call a home.

Next think about colour and forget all the mystique that surrounds this subject. Colour is the most important single ingredient in preparing a successful room scheme, and in itself costs nothing, since you don't have to pay any more for items in attractive colours than in dowdy ones. Once you have developed an eye for colour you will be able to choose and mix colours together with taste and flair to create harmonious schemes which you will find pleasant to live with. The first section will help you with this: it

1

explains the basic principles behind clever colour scheming, tells you how to use colour to create a particular atmosphere and a feeling of space, and how to colour co-ordinate.

Another relevant factor in successful interior decoration is achieving the correct balance between patterned and plain surfaces, and the second section shows you how to mix, match and co-ordinate designs. It is also possible to create illusions with the clever use of pattern: you will discover how easy it is to appear to alter the proportions of a room simply by choosing a certain type of design or a plain colour for the various different surfaces. Selecting the right type of pattern can also help you to decorate a room to create a period style, or a modern atmosphere. Visualising how patterns and plain areas will look in a room is something that some people find particularly difficult, but there are a number of suggestions in this section to help you to cope with this problem.

Texture is the third essential decorating ingredient, since any room looks dull if there is not sufficient textural contrast, even if the colours and the pattern and plain 'mix' are right. This is particularly true if you are planning a scheme made up of mainly plain coloured surfaces: then the texture of each one is vitally important. Texture, like pattern, can also set the style and atmosphere of a room. The third section tells you how to select and blend different textures together skilfully.

But how do you put all this theory into practice? In the final analysis homes are for living in, and as comfortably as possible, so they have to be practical and functional as well as attractive. The second half of the book is devoted to the various main surfaces of a room and tells you what to use where to combine the practical with the pretty. There are also room-by-room ideas for the living, eating and sleeping areas of the home, and finally suggestions for adding accents and accessories, including lighting, to provide those little finishing touches which bring your room schemes to life and stamp your home with your own personality.

4

2

3

TIMOTHY QUALLINGTON

One room three ways – these photographs illustrate the main themes of this book: the successful use of colour, pattern and texture. Although the photographs look completely different, they are in fact the same living room which we decorated in three styles to show how skilful colour scheming and furnishing can create the required effect to suit individual tastes and budgets.

Opposite page: The first room scheme shows how to decorate using plain colour. The clever use of soft greens and browns with white creates a restful effect. The painted wall pattern which echoes the trellis on the upholstery and at the window adds an individual touch to this basic room. The result is a cool, modern room ideal for a young couple with a limited budget.

Above left: The second scheme was designed for a family; the combination of patterned and plain surfaces in warm colours creates an intimate, comfortable atmosphere. The finishes are practical: washable loose covers, wipeable patterned wallcoverings, and loose-laid carpet tiles which can be taken up individually for cleaning.

Below left: The third picture has a totally different appearance – that of an elegant living room suitable for an older couple. The scheme is based on neutral colours, and relies on texture for visual interest. The stone-clad chimney breast provides a focal point, set off by the wool-weave wallcovering in the recesses. Daylight filters through the linen-look vertical blind, enhancing the ripple effect woven in the carpet. The sculptured velvet upholstery fabric links the creams and browns in the room.

Colour sense

The first thing most people notice on entering a room is the colour scheme, because colour creates impact and atmosphere. There are the warm or hot colours like red, orange, tan, gold, pink and yellow, which can be used to make even the coldest room seem warm and cosy, and at the other end of the scale there are the cool or positively cold colours such as blues, greens, blue lilacs, purples, some greys and turquoise. These can help to create a spacious, elegant look (if they are not too dark) in a relatively small area. A third group of colours are often called 'neutral', and include greys (those with some colour content), beiges, creams and off whites, although strictly speaking the only real neutrals are pure black and white, or a mixture of them in varying quantities to create a true grey. This range can be used most successfully to create a balance between several strong or contrasting colours, or alone for a sophisticated tone-on-tone or monochromatic scheme.

The colours we see when we look about us fall into two categories: nature's colours and man-made colours. Natural colours are practically infinite, embracing the numerous greens of grass, trees and foliage; the wide variety of earth colours, ranging from light chalky soil to heavy brown loam; the myriad of colours that the sky alone presents, from the palest haze to deep thunderous purple, or the glowing brilliance of a sunset; and the wide variety found in the flower garden, from the subtlest spring blossoms to the brilliance of poppies and geraniums. Nature rarely makes a mistake when combining colours – think of the perfection of a peacock's tail or a butterfly's wing.

The colours made by man – those that are used for dyeing fibres for textiles; printing paper and wall-coverings; blending paints and inks; and colouring cosmetics and food – are essentially the result of scientific formulæ devised by man, who then has to use his own judgement when combining them. Some people find this an enjoyable and exciting exercise, with pleasing end results; others, however, have great difficulty in using colours successfully.

To understand colour and how to use it creatively you need to learn a little about the fundamentals of colour theory, which is surprisingly simple. It becomes even simpler if you look at the colour wheels on these pages.

Primary, secondary and tertiary colours

All colours originate from the three *primary* colours of red, yellow and blue, which you can see on the first wheel shown opposite. By mixing two primaries together in equal parts you get the three *secondary* colours: red and yellow make orange, for example; blue and yellow make green; and red and blue make violet, as you can see on the second wheel: red, orange, yellow, green, blue and violet. The third wheel consists of the basic range of twelve colours in natural sequence, comprising the three primaries, the three secondaries, and the six *tertiary* colours. These are created when a primary is mixed in equal parts with the secondary colour next to it, making red-orange, yellow-orange, yellow-green, blue-green, blue-violet and red-violet. You will notice on the third colour wheel that the top half consists of the warm or hot colours and the lower half is made up from the cooler ones. The colours opposite each other on the wheel are known as complementary colours, that is red and green, orange and blue, yellow and violet.

All the warm colours are 'advancing' or dominant, and although they can be used very effectively in interior decoration to give a cheerful or intimate atmosphere to a room, they can also make it appear small and claustrophobic. Just one very strong advancing colour in a room can be extremely difficult to live with (and tiring on the eye) if used over a large area without the benefit of contrast. Ideally, hot colours should be combined with some neutral ones, complemented by one of the cooler colours from the opposite side of the wheel, and contrasted with lots of white on the woodwork. Similarly, too many clashing hot colours used together in one room will create a jazzy, bitty effect as the eye jumps from one to another, so again neutrals, white and complementary colours should be introduced.

The cooler colours are known as the 'receding' colours and are much easier to live with, giving even quite a small room a spacious look, but if they are used on their own they can create an unfriendly, often chilly atmosphere. They need to be cheered up with some of the warm, advancing colours on the opposite side of the wheel, but they should also have a neutral link.

Colour terms

Colour in interior decoration is largely involved with, and explained in terms of, pigments and dyes, but there are many words you are likely to come across when reading about the science of colour, and a certain amount of confusion still exists. In an attempt to ensure that we all speak the same language, various methods of describing colour have been devised; however, these names still mean different things to different people.

The technical terms coming into common usage in this country are *hue, lightness/darkness* and *saturation*, and these are the words used throughout this book wherever a technical term is needed to describe colour's properties.

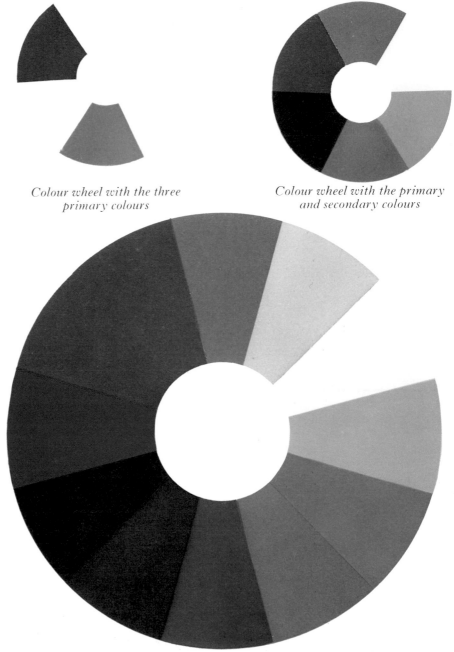

Colour wheel with the three primary colours

Colour wheel with the primary and secondary colours

Colour wheel with the primary, secondary and tertiary colours

Hue is used to describe the six basic colours of the spectrum (red, orange, yellow, green, blue and violet), and is often synonymous with the word colour itself. Hue can also be used to describe mixtures in equal parts of these colours, giving the twelve colours in the wheel shown on page 7.

Really vivid pure colours are very dominant, particularly the warm ones of red, orange and yellow, so these are best used in fairly small quantities in rooms that are lived in all the time and that need to be fairly relaxing. However, these strong colours can be used to great effect in children's rooms, bathrooms, cloakrooms, lavatories and halls, which do not have to be so restful. A contrast should be introduced into such schemes in the form of a clear colour from the opposite side of the wheel.

Lightness/darkness refers to just that factor – the lightness or darkness of a colour, which depends on how much white or black there is in it. For example, pink is a light red, maroon is a dark red.

The light colours reflect light and make a room seem larger and lighter, and the darker ones absorb light, making a room appear smaller and more intimate. It is important to try to have contrasts in a room, although some very effective schemes can be created with subtle lightness changes to make a room seem larger. With such a scheme you will again need to use some vivid splashes of colour – in accents and accessories – from the opposite side of the colour wheel to prevent the room from looking boring.

Saturation (sometimes called colour intensity) describes the strength of a colour and its brightness or dullness, which depends on how much or how little grey there is in it. The smaller the amount of grey a colour contains, the stronger or purer it is said to be, thus rose is a low-saturation red and vermilion is a high-saturation red.

Another accepted method of identifying and describing colours among professional users is called the Munsell System, which was devised in 1915 by Albert Henry Munsell, a painter and art teacher. The salient words used in this system are *hue, value* and *chroma* (or intensity).

The British Standards Institution has done a great deal to standardise the descriptions of colour, and has produced various British Standards to co-ordinate colours so that architects, designers and industry can all operate on the same wave length. They use the words *hue, weight* and *greyness*.

Other words you are likely to come across include:

Monochromatic, meaning literally *mono*: 'one' and *chroma*: 'intensity of colour'. This word is often used to describe the use of different degrees of one colour in a room, varied in lightness and saturation to produce a 'tone-on-tone' scheme, as it is frequently called.

Shade is often used to mean the mixture of a pure hue and varying amounts of black; a shade will harmonise with black.

Tint is often used to mean the mixture of a pure hue and varying amounts of white; a tint will harmonise with white.

Tone is often used to mean the mixture of a shade with white or a tint with black; a tone will harmonise with grey. If you mix black and white together, the result is pure grey, which can vary in lightness depending on the proportions used.

Pastel is the term used to describe a light to medium colour, often a tint with a large proportion of white in it. A pastel can be *muted*, the word used to describe a colour with a high grey content.

Right: The fresh combination of greens in this monochromatic scheme complements the warm tones of the natural wood, and gives the room a spacious appearance.
Far right: A dramatic example of triadic colour harmony: the three primary colours – red, yellow and blue – have been used for the wall painting in this delightful children's playroom. The furniture and woodwork are painted red for extra impact.

BERGER PAINTS

Colour harmony

Many attractive decorating schemes can be achieved by using one of the five 'colour harmonies', and this means going back to the colour wheel. For example, a *triadic colour harmony* is the use of three colours that are an equal distance apart on the wheel, such as red, yellow and blue (the primary colours), red-orange, yellow-green and blue-violet and so on. (A scheme that involves a fourth colour is called a *tetrad*.)

Adjacent colour harmony involves the use of colours that lie next to each other on the wheel (sometimes called *analogous*). Any portion of the wheel can be chosen, but some combinations of colour are more readily acceptable than others, for example yellow harmonises with yellow-orange and yellow-green.

Complementary colour harmony means using colours that are directly opposite each other on the wheel (sometimes called opposite hues), for example red and green or blue-green and red-orange. In this harmony the selection does not have to be too strict, since red and blue can look as good together as red and green, and blue-violet can harmonise with red-orange.

Split-complementary colour harmony occurs when one colour is combined with the two contrasting colours that lie on either side of its complementary colour (directly opposite it on the wheel), for example red-orange with blue and green (a combination frequently found in nature), or orange with blue-violet and blue-green.

Monochromatic colour harmony, as previously described, is when only one colour is used, but varying in lightness and saturation. Rooms decorated in this way need to be combined with either black or white, and should have a few sharp accents introduced in accessories to prevent the scheme from being boring.

NEIL LORRIMER EWA

Basic rules

Having grasped these basic principles you can forget most of the unnecessary mystique surrounding the subject of colour and can enjoy the fun of colour scheming following a few simple rules:

Decorate warm rooms mainly in cool colours.

Decorate small rooms in fairly light colours.

Decorate cold rooms mainly in warm colours.

Decorate large rooms in the richer, darker colours.

Use colours from the opposite ends

The bright blue china ornaments provide the necessary accents to this warm living room scheme based on intense reds and browns.

of the spectrum to balance a scheme, for example burnt orange and turquoise blue, olive green and rose pink, or rich gold and clear sky blue.

Use neutral colours, including white, as a link.

Use vivid splashes of colour as accents in a subtle scheme.

Use pale, cool contrasts with vivid, hot schemes.

A basically simple scheme can be created by using a fairly light colour on the walls, a darker version of the same colour for the floor, with a contrasting (or complementary) colour for the curtains. The upholstery or bedcover could be neutral and all the woodwork a sparkling white. This will be nevertheless effective for being simple. A cool scheme for a living room based on these rules could have pale lime green walls, an olive green carpet, and striped curtains in orange and apricot. The upholstery colour could be a soft peach beige and woodwork and ceiling both painted brilliant white. Colour accents of apricot, orange and strong peacock blue could complete the effect. A warm scheme for a bedroom based on the same rules could have a pastel pink ceiling, slightly paler pink walls and a deep rose pink carpet. The curtains could be patterned in a variety of pinks with emerald green on a white ground and the bedcover and woodwork could be pure white. Accents of deep rose, emerald green and paler mint green could complete the scheme.

This cool scheme based on blue-green walls has sharpest aquamarine on cushions and other accessories. Touches of soft pink provide a warm contrast and sparkling white paintwork offsets the heavy gilt.

Developing an eye for colour

Most people tend not to notice the colour all around them, but in the last few years a revolution has been taking place and superb mouth-watering colour is available to everybody, just waiting to be used. Everything for the home from floorcoverings, textiles, paints and wallcoverings to kitchen units, baths and basins – even simple plastics kitchen containers – now come in an unbelievably wide choice of patterns and colours; we have indeed come a long way from basic Utility furniture and the strident post-war Festival-of-Britain colours.

Colour in itself does not cost anything: you can create a beautiful room scheme without spending any more (often, in fact, considerably less) than you would to produce a dull, dreary one, so it is well worth while learning how to use colour.

But, having assimilated a few basic principles, how do you develop an eye for colour? Some people have a superb natural colour sense while others find it a completely bewildering subject, and there is certainly no precise formula which can be used. The important thing is to throw away any preconceived notions you may have such as: white is always clinical; blue and green should never be seen; or blue is always a cold colour. Approach this fascinating new world with wide-open eyes and, above all, a mind that is receptive to new ideas.

Begin by looking all around you – and this means upwards as well: many people never seem to look above eye level yet quite a lot goes on over our heads. Nature often creates a perfect colour scheme: think of those autumn hues of burnished gold, tans, copper orange, a complete range of browns, with deep rich greens, all contrasted with the clear blue of the sky or the crystal sharpness of a silvery-grey

PHOTOGRAPHS GEORGE F HYDE

Nature can often provide inspiration for a colour scheme.
Top: The colours of this autumnal foliage range from deep spruce green through burnt orange to light gold – all contrasted with the bright blue sky.
Above: Butterflies are among the most highly coloured of nature's creations, many having neutral or plain dark wings highlighted with splashes of bright colours, like this beautiful Peacock settling on ceanothus.

frosty morning; or all the glowing brilliance of a fiery sunset offset by indigo hills deepening to rich purple. Look afresh at a collection of spring flowers: the fragile pastel colours in a bunch of freesias, for example, are offset by verdant green and sunshine yellow. Unfortunately many of these colour combinations cannot be translated into interior decorating schemes because indoors we seldom have the space or quality of light found outside, but it is still possible to look to nature for inspiration when planning a colour scheme.

Once you have started to look around you with greater awareness you will discover there are many other sources of inspiration within easy reach of most of us: for example, an occasional visit to an art gallery or museum; churches and cathedrals can be surprisingly rich in colour too, particularly if there is a quantity of good stained glass. Visiting well furnished stately homes is another fairly obvious way of learning about colour, and about design and decoration as well, for after all the British country house has always been admired and the style is copied throughout the world.

If you do plan to visit museums, galleries, houses and buildings of historic interest, it is always best to try to make a few short colour-and-design-conscious trips rather than trying to assimilate everything in one long intensive visit. Try to study guide books or leaflets in advance (or take them away to look at at home) and then when you go round you will be able to absorb the colour and design principles without getting too bogged down with historical fact. You may wonder whether there is a place for such grandeur in decoration and furnishing today, but even the grandest castle or most superior stately home will be full of ideas which will help you to plan the interior of a modest modern home.

Another way of learning about colour and style of decoration is by watching films that are visually beautiful and historically accurate, particularly if you want to copy a certain period. The sets for many of the plays shown on colour television have done a great deal to increase our awareness of colour and design and can be another source of inspiration.

As well as going out to look, you can learn a lot at home from books on art, decoration and colour; as these are usually expensive the local library would be a good place to start, and then if you find a particular book really helpful you can buy it and keep it for future reference. Features in homemaking and women's magazines; colour pictures used as a background to advertisements; leaflets produced by furniture, fabric, floor- and wall-covering manufacturers: these can all be helpful, so cut out and keep any that take your fancy and you will find you have built up a handy file of ideas fairly quickly.

If all this sounds too much like going back to school, or you simply have not got any time to spare, then it is possible to choose a patterned fabric (for curtains or upholstery) or a multi-coloured wallcovering as a starting point for a decorating scheme. Pick out one colour in the fabric or paper for your floorcovering, another for upholstery, and a third for walls or curtains and contrast these with plenty of sparkling white paintwork. Most of the basic colours can then be used for accessories with the introduction of a complete contrast as an accent colour. If you plan a scheme this way, it is vital that you match your colours exactly to the originals.

NEIL LORRIMER EWA

The floral patterned curtain fabric has been used as the starting point for the colour scheme in this elegant living room. The cool olive green of the leaves is repeated in the carpet, the warm rust-orange upholstery links with the flowers, and the soft sandy-beige wallcovering and paintwork echo the background colour of the curtain fabric.

Colour co-ordinating

Colour can be surprisingly deceptive when used to decorate the different planes of a room, and consequently colour co-ordinating is something not to be undertaken lightly. But it is tremendous fun and also very rewarding when the finished results are successful and a cause for admiration.

Many of the consumer-oriented manufacturers are helping with the problem of colour co-ordinating by producing ranges of complementary wallcoverings and fabrics; carpets that mix and match throughout the house; paint ranges with graded colours; ranges of matching and co-ordinated ceramic and floor tiles; bedroom and bathroom linens and ready-made curtains that blend happily together; roller blinds that match or tone with curtain fabric – the list grows longer weekly. Even with all this help at hand, the actual putting together of colours – and for that matter, the use of patterned and plain surfaces and the mixing of textures in a room – should be approached fairly scientifically.

However colour conscious you are, it is simply not possible to carry colour 'in your eye', and in any case colours change depending on the source, direction and type of light shining on them. All too often, something chosen in so-called daylight lighting in a shop (which in reality is a type of fluorescent light) appears fairly bright or richly coloured. When you get it home in ordinary domestic artificial lighting you may well be disappointed and find it absorbs the light and looks very dull and lifeless. There is only one way to deal with this problem and that is to shop around for colour in a systematic way: don't buy anything on impulse unless it is the first item for a room and you are literally starting the scheme from scratch.

Sampling

If you are using a patterned paper or fabric as the inspiration for your scheme (as suggested opposite), or if you have existing items in the room – such as a carpet, upholstery, curtains, paint or wallcoverings – that you want to incorporate into the new scheme, always take examples with you when you go shopping for new things. Never mind if you are only buying lampshades, accessories or cushions: you still need to be sure they are going to fit happily into the overall scheme.

It is not always practicable to cut a piece off the upholstery fabric or curtains, and we don't all have spare bits of carpet lying around, so it may not be possible to take actual samples, but you can always find pieces of wool, reels of cotton, embroidery silks, bits of ribbon, even pieces of coloured paper to match the things to be included in the new scheme. If desperate, you can always pick up paint manufacturers' colour cards at your local do-it-yourself or decorating shops and colour match to these. Some cards are surprisingly comprehensive, particularly if they are from the type of range that has certain base tints and colourants added to give the different colours. If the existing item is patterned, take samples of all the colours with you when you shop, but also half-close your eyes to get an impression of the predominant colour and take a sample of this too.

When you see something you like and may want to add to your scheme, ask for a sample to add to your collection. Most shops will obtain pieces of carpet, wallcoverings, plastics laminate, kitchen unit colours, tiles and sanitaryware for you; and with fabric for curtains and upholstery (particularly if it is very expensive, or has a large bold design on it), it is usually possible to obtain a large sample from the manufacturer on approval. Incidentally, it is always wise to see as large a sample as possible of a patterned wallcovering, fabric or carpet, so that you can judge more accurately the effect of using it over a large area. If the shop cannot or will not get a sample for you, then you can write direct to the manufacturer, quoting the necessary reference name or number and colourway.

Never, ever, be fobbed off with a leaflet and risk colour matching to this. Unfortunately, colour printing is rarely perfectly true, so you might well be trying to match something to a completely wrong colour. This is equally as true of pictures of kitchen units and worktops; bathroom fittings and tiles; wallcoverings and fabrics; as it is of carpets and floorcoverings. Leaflets and pictures in wallpaper books, however, are very helpful in determining the overall look and scale of a pattern, whether it be on the wall, floor or ceiling or hanging at the window.

Colour boards

As you don't want to be continually searching for the bits and pieces you have gathered together on your trips in search of colour, much the most sensible thing to do is to make a colour board for each room you are planning to decorate. If you enjoy colour matching, or are particularly uncertain about which type of scheme will be suitable, you can make several boards before you finally reach a decision.

Get a piece of stout card – the back of an old stiff envelope would do – and, if you have made a room plan, pin this to the card. If not, then take a note of the measurements of the room, which way it faces, and also measure the window accurately. This will enable you to work out how much curtain fabric you are likely to need should just the right fabric catch your eye during a shopping expedition. Add any other relevant information to the

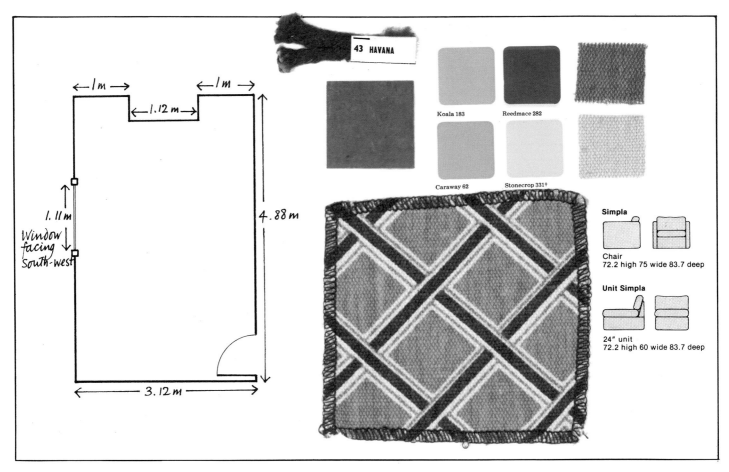

Labels within image:
43 HAVANA
Koala 183
Reedmace 282
Caraway 62
Stonecrop 331†

Simpla
Chair
72.2 high 75 wide 83.7 deep

Unit Simpla
24″ unit
72.2 high 60 wide 83.7 deep

Dimensions on floor plan: 1 m, 1.12 m, 1 m, 1.11 m, 4.88 m, 3.12 m
Window facing South-west

board, such as leaflets of furniture that you already have or may be going to buy, and colour samples of existing items or other suitable colour reference (see above). You are then ready to choose the rest of the colour scheme, adding the samples to your colour board as you go along.

What do you do once the board is complete and you feel you have selected the right merchandise? Hang up the board complete with samples for a few days in the room to be decorated so that you can judge the effect in both artificial and daylight. Also remember to look at things on the plane on which

they will be seen in the room: floorcoverings and upholstery horizontally, wallcoverings and paint for walls vertically, curtain fabric vertically and *against* the light. Lampshades or fabric for them should be seen lit or with light shining through them and table lamp bases with the artificial light shining directly down on them.

Making a colour board also gives the family a chance to participate in choosing a colour scheme and furnishings. It also gives breathing space to work out the budget, and if you keep the board afterwards you will

Colour scheming is simpler if you make a colour board for each room, with its floor plan and samples.

have a record should you need to re-order anything at a later stage. It is also practical to jot down how many rolls of wallpaper were needed, how much paint, the amount of fabric required for curtains and how many square metres of floorcoverings. Then you will have these quantities at your fingertips next time you want to redecorate the room, or tackle a similar one; if you move, the information will be very helpful to the new owners.

Creating space with colour

Colour is an essential ingredient in the creation of a scheme because it helps to give a room atmosphere, but it is also perfectly possible to use colour (and design) to play decorating 'tricks'. By using these skilfully you can actually appear to change the shape and proportions of a room and to disguise faults and enhance good points (see page 40). Much the most common problem these days is that of trying to make a small room look larger, or of giving a spacious feel to a cluttered area where many family activities have to take place. It is feasible to solve the problem partially with the clever choice of colour, but some replanning or pruning may also be necessary, so start by removing non-essential items of furniture and any unnecessary clutter; try and keep your furniture as low and simply shaped as possible.

As I mentioned at the beginning of this section, the cool colours of blue, green, lilac and grey are the receding ones, and so this is the group from which to choose your scheme if you want to create a feeling of space. Colours vary in intensity too, so a pale, dull (or subtle) colour will be much less dominant than a clear, bright one, so again choose the paler, more subtle colours as opposed to the strong, vivid ones if you want an illusion of increased space.

Of course, if the room is cold you will not want to decorate it with chilly

Pale colours and a mirror give an illusion of increased space in this attic bedroom.

colours, so try to use very pale colours like pastel pink, apricot, lightest primrose, or one of the neutrals such as soft beige, cream or off white (more about these on page 24). Remember, too, that these pale colours, and in particular white, have a high reflective value and the more light you can bring into the room the greater will be the apparent size. In a really dark area, such as a narrow hall or a room with a very small window, a cleverly placed mirror or a wall of mirror tiles will often double the amount of reflected light, at the same time making the room appear much larger.

If the eye is forced to jump about from surface to surface in a room, the overall 'bitty' effect makes it seem much smaller (as do strong patterns), and so the ideal scheme for a tiny, dark room is one which is based on several versions of a pale, cool colour. Keep the majority of the surfaces plain, or at most introduce only one small mini-print or other scarcely defined pattern, to be used discreetly. For example, a small box-like living room could be carpeted in a very pale sage green, all the walls painted a light greeny silver and the woodwork and ceiling picked out in a brilliant white. The curtains might be striped in soft grey-greens on a white ground and pale silver upholstery could complete the scheme. Any warm accents introduced in accessories would be best chosen from the apricot and tangerine range.

In a small bedroom, with sloping ceilings and very little daylight coming through a small skylight, walls and sloping ceiling could be covered with a paper patterned with tiny lilac and pale blue shadowy flowers on a white ground; the flat part of the ceiling painted a toning pale blue; the woodwork picked out in white; the carpet might be a pale lilac and the scheme completed with a white bedcover and white furniture.

A similar balance, this time of pale blues and greens, could be used to make a living room or a bedroom appear more spacious, but if you have to start with a cold room, and are choosing your colours from the warmer range, you might use light lemon on the walls with a soft gold carpet and upholstery for a living room, or a mixture of palest apricot and lime, or sugared-almond pinks for a bedroom scheme.

Using white as the main non-colour in a scheme does, of course, make a room appear much larger and lighter, particularly if the walls are covered with a textured paper or vinyl which is slightly shiny – say a foil, silk or moiré effect. A matt, white-painted ceiling and glossy white woodwork will further enhance the light, spacious look, but the scheme might be too clinical or – worse – it could be boring. So the remaining surfaces must be chosen with care. To warm it up a bit, add a soft golden-beige carpet with a longish pile and curtains in a textured weave in golden-brown stripes on white. Add slightly deeper golden-brown upholstery and warm yew, maple or pine furniture and the result will be spacious and elegant. A little soft turquoise used as an accent colour would further enhance the scheme.

How to use warm colours

Where and how do you use warm colours for maximum effect, and what goes with what to create a balanced scheme? If you look back to the colour wheels illustrated on page 7, you will see that one half consists of the warm or hot colours, ranging from the warm plum purples, through deep pink, reds, orange and orange gold to yellow and golden green.

Strong red is the warmest colour of all, closely followed by orange; golds; most yellows (unless they have a strong touch of green); deep pink; apricots; rich browns; tans; most of the range of autumnal colours; lilac pinks; rose pink; warm beiges and creams. Many natural surfaces have a pleasing warmth of their own too: wood used for flooring and wall-cladding as well as for furniture; most brick and terracotta ceramics; cork in all its versions from brownish black to honey gold; the soft creamy colours of wool (in carpets and furnishing fabrics); sisals and rush mattings; rattan and cane; these can all be used to add extra warmth to a scheme (see the section on textures).

The significance of the terms hot and warm when applied to colour becomes more apparent when the aspect and size of a room is being taken into consideration before planning a colour scheme. For example, a room that faces north and does not enjoy direct sunlight is likely to be cold and uninviting. Similarly, a room that is overshadowed by large trees or tall buildings is also bound to be cold whichever way it faces (and probably dark into the bargain), and basement or semi-basement rooms nearly always have a distinctly chilly atmosphere. A room that faces east may get the early morning sun, but it too is likely to be cold for a greater part of the day. All these rooms are those where you can use the warm or even hot colours to give them a cheerful, cosy atmosphere.

Remember, however, when choosing colours from the warm side of the wheel: the nearer the colour is to the original primary, the stronger it will be in intensity, and the more advancing – and consequently harder to live with. Very strong, bright, hot colours should, in the main, be used with discretion – on small areas, or as accents or in accessories. Of course, if you want to experiment with vivid colour you can do so, but it is wiser to use it on a surface that is fairly easy to change: wallpaper or paint for the walls, for example, which can be quickly altered with a flick of the paint brush or sweep of the roller and a new pot of paint.

If you have to decorate a very large, chilly room; a tall hall, stair and landing area in a Victorian house; or a large through-room where two rooms have been knocked into one or a sizeable extension has been added; stronger colours can be used on several surfaces. The cold hall, for example, might have an apricot-coloured ceiling with a white cornice, most of the walls painted a strong burnt orange or terracotta, the wall at the side of the stairs papered with a washable wallcovering patterned in brown, orange, apricot and white, with sparkling white woodwork and a rich brown carpet throughout. But remember the golden rule about adding a cool colour from the other side of the wheel to bring the scheme to life – a vivid jade green or strong turquoise blue would look particularly effective used for curtains and some of the accessories. The long living room would look very cosy with a rich gold carpet, walls striped in gold and white with a white ceiling and woodwork and ruby red velvet curtains; the white provides a contrast, but olive green could be added to the scheme in upholstery fabric, with some sharper lime green used, together with olive, red, gold and white, and some brass for the finishing touches.

When the cold room is tiny, you have to ask yourself whether you want to try and make it cosy and intimate or whether such a scheme would be overpowering and claustrophobic. In the main, small, dark rooms look best decorated in a range of warm colours which are less intense. A smallish dining room would look fresh and spring like if the walls and ceiling were painted primrose yellow, the carpet was a light tan and curtains were printed in yellow and tangerine on a white ground; white and some pale turquoise could provide colour contrast in tableware and other accessories. In a small, square bedroom, the scheme could be based on a soft rose carpet, with three walls and ceiling painted a pale rose to tone, and the woodwork picked out in an even paler pink. The curtain fabric and the paper on the bedhead wall might be printed with the same mini-design in rose, pink and lime green on white – the lime providing the accent colour.

Bathrooms in particular are usually very small, and frequently face north. If a coloured suite and tiles are being chosen they have to be easy to live with, since once installed they are permanent fixtures. This is one of the rooms where a spacious atmosphere is not necessarily required, but if it is, tricks can be played with mirror to make it appear larger. For a really cosy effect, the bath and sanitaryware could be deep plum, with tiles to tone, a strong pink long-pile carpet on the floor and a pink/plum paper on the walls above the tiles. The ceiling and woodwork might echo the pink of the carpet. A little Wedgwood blue used as an accent colour with some brilliant white could complete the scheme. A lighter, more spacious effect would be gained if the bath and wash basin were in a soft apricot; the walls could be covered with a simple patterned tile in apricot, white and soft milky chocolate. The ceiling and woodwork would look effective in either apricot or the milky-chocolate colour and a deep bitter-chocolate floorcovering could complete the scheme.

SPIKE POWELL EWA

BERGER PAINTS

SCHONER WOHNER

The photographs on these pages illustrate the use of warm colours to create a cheerful atmosphere.
Opposite page: Various pinks are contrasted with touches of Prussian blue in this attractive living room.
Above left: A dramatic treatment of the kitchen in an Edwardian mansion flat. Brilliant scarlet gloss paint has been used liberally – even on the cooker.
Left: Sunshine yellow on one wall in this study is echoed on the painted chair and checked roller blind.

Above: Deep rust paint on the walls and supporting joist complement the natural finishes of the wood units and cork floor to create a stylish kitchen/dining room.

How to use cool colours

Which are the cool or cold colours? These are the ones on the opposite side to the warm and hot colours on the colour wheel (see page 7). They start with bluish purples and go through all the blues, blue-greens, greens and some of the yellow-greens to the greeny golds. Most lilacs are cold until they begin to show a hint of pink; greys (unless they have a lot of pink or yellow mixed with them); some of the beiges (the greeny or blue beiges); these are all cool colours, and of course so are black and white (strictly speaking these are non-colours).

Once again the aspect and size of the room will determine whether you use cool colours or not, and how intense they are. Rooms that face directly south, west or south-west and enjoy the full afternoon sun are likely to seem naturally warm, even in the depth of winter (if the sun is shining), so they can take any of the cooler colours in the spectrum. Pale, cool colours are ideal for warm rooms overlooking a garden, or for conservatories and extensions where you want to create a feeling of space and light and are aiming to link the area visually with the garden. They look very effective too in a room where most of the accessories are provided by a collection of house plants. Green in particular suits the above situations, but it can also bring a country freshness to a dull city room. A hot, steamy kitchen is an ideal place to use the range of cool or cold colours, and they can also look marvellous in small, poky bedrooms – particularly in attics or in chalet bungalows with sloping ceilings, which can both become oppressively hot in summer.

As with the warm colours, the closer the cold colour is to the original primary, the stronger it will be in intensity – a brilliant blue for example, or a strong purple or a vivid green will all be fairly difficult to live with unless they are tempered with a lot of white, mixed with some paler cool colours and contrasted with touches of warmth. And again, unless you are very sure of your colour-scheming abilities, use the really bold, strong colours on an area that is fairly easy to change.

Blue can be a tricky colour to use in interior decoration, and should only be used in large quantities in a really light, warm, sunny room, but if cleverly handled, blue can give a scheme an exotic Mediterranean feeling. If it is to be successful as a colour scheme at night, it needs plenty of warm artificial lighting (no steely glare); in fact blue always needs plenty of good flexible lighting. Several different blues mixed together in one room can make a really exciting tone-on-tone scheme and blue also mixes well with most of the warm colours. Try it with creams and browns; with orange, apricot and terracotta; with pinks and reds; with purples and lilacs; with golds and tans; and it can look really stunning with scarlet, so long as there is plenty of white in the scheme.

Pale blues, because they look like a cloudless sky, can give the impression of endless space: a pale sky-blue or turquoise paint used on the ceiling of a low room can make it appear much taller. For a really elegant blue living room, paint all the walls a strong cornflower blue, with the ceiling and doors in a turquoise and the cornice and other woodwork in a soft cream; carpet with a creamy-white wool carpet with a long pile; curtain with a patterned chintz in mixed blues on a cream ground and for the upholstery use a soft milky-chocolate corded velvet. Complete the scheme with accessories in all the blues, creams and milky chocolate with some coral used as an accent colour; this scheme would work well in a fairly large or medium-sized room but would be too overpowering in a small one.

Green is easier to use than many colours because so many greens blend together happily and you only have to look at nature for inspiration. Green used to be considered an unlucky colour for clothes and decoration – a superstition which goes back for hundreds of years and which probably arose because the vegetable dye used to make green cloth contained a poison which affected the dyers. Happily this is no longer the case and this strange superstition, together with the myth that all blues fade and the saying 'blue and green should never be seen', has been swept away.

As green is such a refreshing colour, it is ideal for a kitchen, combined with pine furniture or wood-grain units and worktops, or in a bathroom mixed with rose and white and accessorised with steam-loving house plants. A very bright, strong green can give a modern living room a cool, sophisticated atmosphere when offset with simple white furniture and some chrome or stainless steel and smoked glass pieces. Green, in its paler and more subtle forms, can also be a very relaxing decoration colour and very easy to live with. Imagine a high-ceilinged sunny bedroom in a Victorian house, furnished with some rather heavy mahogany furniture. The ceiling could be painted a pale golden green with the cornice picked out in white, the walls papered with a William Morris *art nouveau* flowing floral wallpaper in greens with a little soft apricot and deeper burnt orange, and the woodwork painted shiny white. The curtains could be in apricot silk, trimmed with green braid and held back with green tie-backs, over a roller blind in fabric to match the wallpaper, and a deep olive green carpet and a white lace or crocheted bedcover could complete the scheme.

Blue and green can be used very effectively together in a scheme, and in fact all the cold colours blend together in a much more satisfactory way than the warm ones. It is possible to create a really sensational scheme based on deep purple, lilac, lime and olive green, peacock and turquoise blue contrasted with white. To achieve a balanced effect you need to be careful with the choice of the different versions of the various colours. For example, if you plan to decorate a child's nursery in a mixture of cool colours, the floor could be tiled with dark and light blue tiles laid chequerboard fashion; the ceiling painted in the same light blue; three walls painted a strong lime green, with the fourth wall devoted to a notice board and blackboard area (the notice board might be covered in dark green felt); the woodwork in white with the doors in the same lime as the walls; curtains in a patterned fabric in blues, greens, purples and lilacs on a white ground; and to furnish the room use whitewood furniture with white-painted carcasses and drawers, and doors painted in lime, light blue and purple. As you need to introduce some warmth into the scheme when you are decorating with mainly cool colours, a little hot Siamese pink could complete this room.

Greys, black and white, and some beiges are also classed as cold or cool colours, but these are also considered to be neutrals, so suggestions for using them are given here.

The photographs on these pages show four ways of using cool colours successfully.
Left: Our first living room scheme (see page 4) is based on pale greens and natural browns with lots of white, creating a cool, spacious atmosphere.
Below: A painted mural can add an amusing extra dimension to a child's

DAVID CRIPPS

room. This fantasy world covers both wall and sloping ceiling, yet the use of cool colours prevents it from being overpowering.
Above right: The wall tiles in this charming, old-fashioned bathroom combine cool colours of blue, green, grey, lilac and purple. The lavender and lilac towels provide the accents.
Right: A mixture of strong greens gives this modern bathroom impact. The monochromatic scheme is relieved by touches of red and white.

JESSICA STRANG

JESSICA STRANG

How to use neutral colours

This group of colours is not shown on the colour wheel, because they are not, strictly speaking, colours of the spectrum, but they are created by mixing white and black (or grey) with a hue until a pale neutral is produced. They are mostly fairly light and include the greys, off whites, creams and beiges; black and white are also neutral (see page 26).

As the greys, creams and beiges can be either warm (those based on yellow, orange and red) or cold (those based on green, blue and violet), they can be difficult colours to blend together and need to be chosen even more skilfully than many of the brighter colours of the spectrum. It is no use thinking that because a colour is a neutral it will automatically go harmoniously with other neutrals. If you plan to base a scheme on greys, off whites or beiges, you will need to make a colour board (see page 14) and select colours with just as much (and probably more) care and attention as you would for a bright, bold scheme.

Despite this, many people still prefer to choose the more neutral colours for most of their furnishings, and certainly neutrals can be very beautiful, introducing a calm, restful effect and helping to create a feeling of space. They lend themselves particularly well to monochromatic (tone-on-tone) schemes which look very elegant and spacious, but clever colour co-ordination is imperative if they are to be a success.

Beige is probably the most continuously popular neutral: a beige carpet has been the starting point for many a decorating scheme because it helps to give the room a light, airy look, does not show the dirt too much and at the same time manages to look expensive and luxurious. Don't use a beige carpet in a dingy or dark room unless you mix it with plenty of sparkling white, but in a light living room you could paint the walls and ceiling slightly darker than the carpet; pick out the woodwork in a creamy white; curtain with a soft coffee-beige velvet and for the upholstery have covers patterned in brown, coffee, beige and cream. This sophisticated scheme would then need a few accents added in accessories to emphasise the monochromatic effect: jade green, turquoise, peach or coral would all provide the right contrast – the first two if you wanted a basically cool scheme, the last two if you prefer a warm scheme.

Grey is probably the next most popular neutral, and can be used very effectively with black and white. In a modern dining room, furnished with chrome and smoked acrylic table and chairs and white wall units with smoked glass doors, the floor could be tiled in black and white; one wall papered with a pattern or mural effect in black, white and grey; the remaining walls and ceiling painted soft grey to tone; with white coving and woodwork. This would be a basically neutral room which might then be given a different curtain and accessory treatment for autumn and winter when extra warmth is needed – red or orange could be very effectively introduced into the scheme. In spring and summer, when a cooler look was required, the curtains could be removed and white vertical blinds hung in their place; accessories could be in sharp lime and emerald green, or blue, purple and lilac.

Neutral colour schemes adapt themselves very easily to seasonal changes, and it is often practical to use the neutrals for the main surfaces in a room: floor, walls, ceiling and woodwork, and to change the window treatment and accessories to suit the season. Loose covers in a pretty floral fabric can be put on the upholstered furniture during the spring and summer and removed to expose a warmer, cosy tweed fabric in autumn and winter. If it is possible to alter the position of the furniture as well – sofas and/or chairs grouped near the fireplace or heater during the winter and facing the window and garden during the summer – this gives a home greater flexibility and interest and at the same time evens out the wear on floorcoverings and helps preserve the upholstery, if loose covers are used for part of the year.

Grey can also be used to create a very restful atmosphere in a bedroom: for a traditional scheme, the walls could be papered with silver-grey stripes on a white moiré ground, the ceiling painted a lighter grey and the woodwork slightly darker; the carpet might be a mixture of these greys with white. To ring the seasonal changes, curtains and bedcover could be a warm rose pink for winter and a deep lilac for summer.

Neutrals can also put a brake on a riotously colourful scheme which may be running away with itself. They can provide a contrast or a link between the various areas of the room; for example, most dark or richly coloured surfaces look better if they are offset by sparkling white, soft off white or creamy woodwork. The choice of neutral will depend on the main colours used in the scheme: white looks best as a link or contrast to bright greens, reds, blues, purples, all the intense colours near to the original primaries; cream is a perfect foil for dark brown, burnt orange, terracotta and tangerine; and off white contrasts well with olive green, golds and the golden greens. If it is a slightly pinky off white (for example, magnolia), then it will be particularly effective with reds, plums and pinks. Very pale grey can be used in the same way to contrast or link with bold colours, and again a fairly pure, clear silver grey would look best with the bolder primary colours; a soft grey with a hint of yellow in it could be used with the autumnal colours and a pinky grey be used with the red/plum/pink group.

A word about white as a neutral: there are actually many different whites, and if you have a white carpet (which in reality is probably off white), white unit furniture or white curtains, and you decide to use one of the sparkling or 'brilliant' white paints now available for your woodwork, you may get a shock. This white paint – particularly if it is in a gloss finish – could make your carpet, furniture or curtains look distinctly dirty. If you already have white items in the room it is wise to match all other whites very carefully to them.

These photographs show three entirely different room schemes, based on three groups of neutral colours.

Left: A dramatic effect is achieved in this modern dining room by the use of neutrals in the grey range – black and white floor tiles and furniture, bold grey painted design on one white wall – all highlighted by touches of chrome.

Right: At first glance this elegant bedroom scheme does not look neutral, but the basic decorations are off white with natural wood for the floor and furniture. The rich pink bedcover provides a striking focal point, adding the necessary warm accent colour.

Below right: Our third living room scheme (see page 5) uses the beige range of neutrals for a monochromatic effect. The subtly patterned upholstery fabric links the warm neutral colours, and the turquoise cushions and accessories introduce a cool contrast.

TIMOTHY Qf ALLINGTON

27

Pattern and plain

Successful room schemes do not rely on colour alone, even though the first section of this book is devoted entirely to the subject of colour. Pattern and texture play an essential part too and must be chosen as carefully as the colours and blended together with equal skill. They should be introduced into a scheme to give contrast and an extra visual dimension, and although you will want to mix and match patterned and plain surfaces to create a certain effect, the plain surfaces will not necessarily be perfectly plain and matt – they will probably have textural interest. In the next section you can see the various different types of texture which are available for use in interior decoration.

Just as colour can make a room appear warm and cosy, cool and spacious, bright and gay, or quiet and relaxing; so the mixture of patterned and plain surfaces can help to create a certain mood in a room, making it relaxed and casual, traditional and formal, stimulating and exciting, or restful and soothing. Pattern, and to some extent texture also, sets the style of a room in a way which colour alone cannot do, and whether you are planning to create a traditional or modern scheme, the designs which you use on certain areas will have to 'feel' right if the room is to have the correct period or modern flavour (see page 46). The clever use of patterned and plain surfaces, combined with the successful choice of colour, can appear to alter the proportions of a room and will also help to correct ugly architectural faults and enhance good points; on page 40 you can see some ideas to help you improve room proportions using pattern.

But what exactly is pattern? It can be a linear design printed on wallcoverings, floorings and curtains; or a design woven into carpets and fabrics; it can even be painted with a brush on a wall or furniture, in the form of wall patterns, *trompe l'oeil* effects and murals.

Pattern is also made by separate objects grouped together: ceramic tiles, for example, when used on a wall or on the floor can form a distinct pattern even though they may be plain or have only a simple textured surface. Carpet or linoleum tiles can be laid to create a definite chequerboard, herringbone or other distinctive design, but plain-coloured carpet tiles laid at right angles to each other can also form a pattern as the light catches the different directions of the pile. Books on shelves; light filtering through the slats of a Venetian blind or through a coloured or obscured glass window; a group of pictures on a wall or a collection of objects on a shelf or table; the positioning of furniture; the hand rail, banisters and open treads of a staircase; the grouping of cushions on a sofa or divan – these all form some sort of pattern even if they are mostly plain in themselves, so this juxtaposition of one material with another must also be considered in relation to pattern when planning the overall room scheme.

How much pattern should you use in a room, and where? The first thing to consider is the atmosphere you want to create. If you intend to have a fairly restful living room or bedroom scheme, then the pattern you choose should be fairly unobtrusive; you might use a small mini-print wallcovering on all the walls, but this will tend to look like an interestingly textured, rather than an obviously patterned surface. Instead you might prefer to use a design on the curtain fabric and keep the other surfaces plain; somehow patterned curtain fabric tends to look less obvious than pattern on a wallcovering, even if they are both printed with the same design. The fact that curtains hang in

TIMOTHY QUALLINGTON

Our second living room scheme (see page 5) *shows the successful use of patterned and plain furnishings. The curtains, blind and cushion covers made up in a neat geometric patterned fabric are set against one of two companion wallcoverings. Toning plain upholstery and cushion covers pick out the colours in the patterned fabric. Note how different the same patterned fabric looks on the flat plane of the roller blind than when hanging in folds.*

ceilings, the walls and sloping area might well be papered with a pretty flowing floral design to create a country cottage atmosphere. The companion patterned fabric could well be used for curtains and bedcover, teamed with a plain carpet, plain upholstered chair with a scatter cushion covered in the curtain fabric, and emulsion paint for the flat part of the ceiling. In a stark modern living room one area of wall could be painted with a dramatic wall pattern, and a similar geometric theme might be printed on the curtain fabric, which should completely cover one wall of window. The flooring could be cleverly chosen to link the two together: light and dark carpet tiles (echoing the colours on the wall and at the window), possibly laid chequerboard fashion. Some of the upholstery in such a scheme could be patterned, so long as it also has a geometric design, and is smaller in scale than either wall or window, with the other upholstery in a really interesting texture such as a nubbly tweed, canvas or a luxurious leather.

The practical aspect must also be considered when choosing patterned and plain surfaces. If a room is to be used by a family that includes children and/or pets, a patterned carpet or other floorcovering is a good starting point. If you don't care for a patterned carpet, you should at least compromise

luxurious folds on each side of the window during the daytime and in generous gathers when drawn across the window at night, gives the fabric a greater fluidity than its static counterpart, the wallcovering.

If you prefer to create a lively, stimulating atmosphere, then you can use pattern in greater profusion on walls, curtains, floorcovering and upholstery, but the effect would be very 'busy' indeed. In such a room the surfaces would need co-ordinating carefully, the designs should each be in a different scale and the pattern

must be of a similar type – either all floral or all geometric, for example. You can, of course, combine simple stripes and checks with other types of pattern, whether it be modern or traditional, floral or geometric, small or large. Often a stripe or a check can provide a link in a scheme between patterns of different sizes or types.

Balance between pattern and plain
In a well balanced scheme probably two, or at the very most three, surfaces would be patterned; in an attic or chalet bungalow bedroom with sloping

29

This spectacular collection of old ceramic wall tiles blend well together as they are similar in style. They also link with the row of art nouveau *tiles on the traditional washstand.*

treatment. This could again be combined with one of the 'textural-interest' types of carpet.

Pattern is similar to colour in some ways: strong patterns advance, while small designs recede so that they look almost plain when seen from a distance; consequently a bold design on walls, door, curtains or furniture is much harder to live with than a plain or textured surface. It is also sensible to confine bold design to the surfaces that are fairly easy and inexpensive to change. A patterned wallcovering, for example, can easily be stripped off and replaced with a completely different design or texture; most types can also be overpainted in emulsion with a large brush or roller. Patterned loose covers or bedcovers can be alternated with plain to give a room a new look (you can make this a seasonal change), and curtains can be altered to fit other windows, or even dyed.

There are several places in the house where you definitely don't want 'busy' designs, or for that matter harsh, strong colours: on kitchen work surfaces, where patterns can actually cause eye strain and will bore you stiff after a month's preparing food on them; on bathroom tiles, where the design will limit you to future colour and furnishing schemes until in desperation you try to cover them up (not easy unless you resort to wood cladding the entire room) or hack them off and start again. Similarly, a very bold design on a carpet, particularly if it is laid throughout the ground floor of a house and up the stairs onto the landing, can appear to come up and 'hit you in the eye' every time you open the front door.

and, instead of using a perfectly plain velvet-pile carpet, select a simple tweedy or tri-tone effect, in which several different versions of the same colour (or contrasting colours) are woven together to create a textured look. Upholstery in such rooms also needs to be practical; if you have opted for a fairly busily patterned floorcovering, then washable, or at least wipeable plain chair covers will be essential. If you decide on the tweedy look for the flooring, then removable, patterned, washable loose covers could well be the answer. In a large hall, where the walls take a lot of punishment from small sticky fingers (particularly the wall at the side of the stairs), a patterned, washable vinyl wallcovering would be a practical

Two traditional rooms where pattern is confined to the soft furnishings, and set off by plain walls.
Below: The formal floral-patterned carpet blends happily with the chintz loose covers in this basically cool, neutral scheme.
Below right: A warm, intimate atmosphere has been created here by the use of a variety of patterns, all with the same ethnic feeling.

SPIKE POWELL

JESSICA STRANG

How to visualise

Most people start a decorating scheme with a carpet or several pieces of upholstered furniture, and whether these are already an integral part of the furnishings or whether you are starting from scratch, it is often easier to make such items a jumping-off point, as the range of wallcoverings, paints and curtain fabrics is so vast today that it is almost always possible to find something that will blend and tone with existing floorcoverings or soft furnishings. Carpets in particular are now a very expensive item in the household budget, and so is that status symbol the three-piece suite. All too often a brightly coloured and boldly patterned carpet or upholstery fabric is mistakenly chosen 'because it won't show the dirt' and you are then forced to live for many years with an expensive misfit, because you can't afford to change it.

Often an expensive error is made because of the problem many people have with visualising – translating the effect of a small sample onto a large area of wall, floor or furniture. It is difficult to make any hard and fast rules about visualising, but it helps to remember that rich colours and strong designs will look much bolder when seen over a large expanse of wall or completely covering a vast area of floor. Conversely, pale colours and tiny patterns tend to fade into insignificance when used over a large area. Large designs or very strong ones also make a room look smaller and can create a definite hemmed-in or oppressive atmosphere in a medium-sized or small room. The smaller patterns and lighter-looking designs can make a room seem more spacious and bright.

Before buying any furnishings with a strong pattern, try to see as large a sample as you can. With a carpet it is usually possible to select from a shop which stocks rolls of a narrow width or pieces of the wider broadloom carpet. Ask to see any patterned carpet unrolled so that you can judge the effect, and with linear carpet have two rolls placed side by side so that you can see how the design links from width to width. If you are ordering a floorcovering from a small sample, try to see a picture of the overall design, but never use a leaflet or picture for colour matching, as colour printing is unfortunately rarely accurate.

Most wallcovering manufacturers take pictures of many of their designs used on two or three walls in a room setting, and you will find that these are interleaved between the pages of pattern books. You will be able to look at these as you go through the book, and judge the effect of the various designs from the lithos (as these pictures are called), even if they are not in the colourway of your choice. In a shop that has lots of rolls in stock it may be possible to undo two rolls and to place them vertically next to each other to see how the design will look; try to unroll enough to give you an idea of the complete drop (the measurement between the ceiling or picture rail and the skirting board in *your* room).

Some manufacturers also produce leaflets or helpful booklets showing their wallcovering designs in room settings, and again you can use these as a guide to visualising the completed room; you will find pictures in books and magazines equally helpful.

If it is your first attempt at decoration, and you really feel unsure of your ability to use colour, patterned and plain surfaces and textures together successfully, you could do worse than copy an attractive room from a current magazine or manufacturer's leaflet – you will usually find full details of the various products are given, unless it is a room in a private home. Several of the wallcovering and paint manufacturers also run decoration advisory services and will be delighted to give you a helping hand and a complete scheme. Some firms make a charge for this service, while others give advice free; samples and full merchandising notes are provided.

When buying curtain fabric, you should again ask to see enough fabric unrolled to judge the full effect of the pattern; look at it vertically and with two widths side by side and preferably the same drop (curtain track to floor measurement) as your window. If, however, you are ordering the fabric from a swatch, you should be able to borrow a largish sample about one metre long by a full width, on sale or return or on approval. The fabric supplier, upholsterer or curtain maker should be able to organise this for you.

Once you have decorated a few rooms, you will find that the problem of visualising becomes much easier – it is definitely something that can be learnt fairly quickly, but if in doubt, rather than playing safe and creating a rather dull scheme, use any bold pattern on a surface, such as the wall, that is fairly easy to change.

When choosing patterned materials, particularly large-scale designs, it helps to see them in use (either in a showroom or in a photograph), rather than relying on a small sample to give the overall effect. Here a large pear design on the wallcovering is repeated on the roller blinds and cushions. It does not overpower the room because it is printed in one colour only, and the paintwork, furniture and floorcovering are plain to link with the off-white background of the design.

33

How to mix and match

How much pattern to use is always a problem; tastes have changed recently and co-ordinated ranges of wallcoverings and fabrics have made it possible to mix and match much more easily. However, if you follow the principle that one strong design can kill another, a scheme is likely to be much more successful if you use only two, or at the most three, patterns in a room; two of them should be specifically co-ordinated and the other could be simple stripes or checks – don't try to use three completely unrelated designs in the same room.

You will find pattern breaks down roughly into three types: florals, bold geometrics and the more neutral stripes, checks and abstracts. Florals can be used together successfully, so can geometrics (see page 44) but the two types of design do not mix together very successfully; the neutrals can be used with either to help create a balance. There are also some specifically traditional patterns available on wallcoverings, curtain fabric and carpets, which you would need to use if you were planning a particular period decor (see page 46) and there are Oriental, Indian and other designs which would give a distinctive foreign flavour to a scheme.

In the 1960s there was a popular trend towards different wall treatments in the same room: frequently one wall was patterned (often called the feature wall), while the other three were papered with an interesting texture in one of the colours in the patterned paper, or occasionally they were emulsion painted in a colour to tone, over a textured woodchip or Anaglypta surface. Sometimes the process was reversed and the feature wall was painted in a rich colour with a patterned paper used on the other three walls, again coloured to link with the plain wall. This treatment was developed because so many houses built in the 1950s and 1960s had box-like rooms, and the mixture of patterned and plain walls in one room made it look much more interesting.

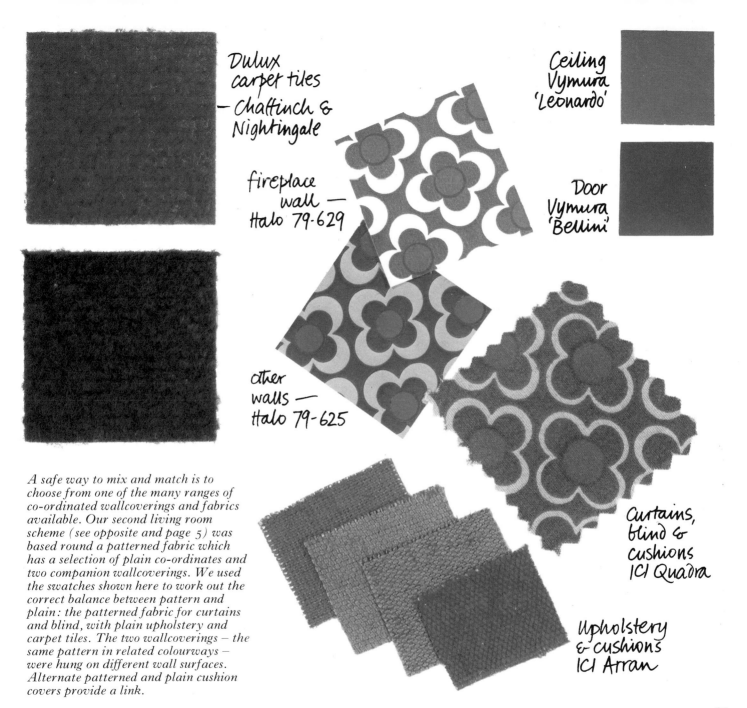

Dulux
carpet tiles
— Chaffinch &
Nightingale

fireplace
wall —
Halo 79-629

other
walls —
Halo 79-625

Ceiling
Vymura
'Leonardo'

Door
Vymura
'Bellini'

Curtains,
blind &
cushions
ICI Quadra

Upholstery
& cushions
ICI Arran

A safe way to mix and match is to choose from one of the many ranges of co-ordinated wallcoverings and fabrics available. Our second living room scheme (see opposite and page 5) was based round a patterned fabric which has a selection of plain co-ordinates and two companion wallcoverings. We used the swatches shown here to work out the correct balance between pattern and plain: the patterned fabric for curtains and blind, with plain upholstery and carpet tiles. The two wallcoverings – the same pattern in related colourways – were hung on different wall surfaces. Alternate patterned and plain cushion covers provide a link.

In the living room it was usually the fireplace wall that was treated differently and in the bedroom, the bedhead wall – a good place to put patterned paper as you can't see it when you are sitting up in bed. Although this is regarded as slightly old fashioned these days, there is no reason why you should not mix and match in this way if the room is large enough to take such a treatment; apart from making a square room look more interesting, it is a good way of decorating a long room to make it seem wider (see page 40).

If you want to use this type of one-wall-patterned, three-walls-plain treatment, then it is sensible to keep most of the other surfaces plain; if you have a patterned paper on the bedhead wall with three plain walls, then you might use a companion fabric for curtains, or for the bedcover, with a plain or two-tone carpet. In a living room with one wall painted a rich dark colour and the other walls papered in a geometric pattern, the carpet could match the feature wall, curtains could be striped in the same colour on a neutral ground and the plain upholstery might be fairly light, echoing one of the colours in the wallpaper. This contrasting wall treatment is also particularly successful for large, unwelcoming entrance halls of the type found in Victorian and Edwardian houses: use a very bold design in strong, warm colours on the wall at the side of the stairs, and paint the other walls to match one of the colours in the wallcovering. Pick out a pale colour from the wallcovering for the ceiling and paint cornices or covings and mouldings in white, also paint most of the woodwork white, except for the doors, which can echo a darker colour in the feature wall. The carpet could be in the three colours of ceiling, walls and doors woven together.

This type of pattern-and-plain mixing can be used very successfully to make a three-piece suite look more attractive and flexible. Personally I would never give a suite of sofa and two chairs house room – unit seating, separate chairs or two sofas and occasional chairs give a room a much more varied and interesting seating arrangement. But if you have a sofa and matching chairs you might re-cover or loose-cover the sofa in a patterned material to match the curtains, and the two chairs could be in contrasting plain fabric picking up colours from the patterned cover and curtains. Scatter cushions could be mixed and matched in the plain and patterned fabric to link the furnishing scheme further.

Similar patterned-and-plain treatments can look very effective at large windows, or where there is a radiator under the window which makes long curtains impractical in the winter. There are many patterned and plain roller blinds available now (and roller blind kits to roll your own), and some have companion or co-ordinated fabrics and wallcoverings. A patterned roller blind to the sill, with long curtains in a plain, toning fabric can look fabulous, particularly if the blind matches the wallcovering.

In a scheme that looks rather plain when it is finished because perhaps the only pattern in the room has been used on the carpet or curtain fabric, it is possible to create an area of pattern using accessories. On a plain sofa, for example, you could group a selection of scatter cushions: some could be in a patterned fabric to match the curtains, one or two might be embroidered tapestry or *petit point*, with perhaps a patchwork one for contrast and several plain ones. If the walls look too stark, then you could mass a selection of prints, pictures and other objects on a plain wall above a sofa or sideboard

(include a mirror or a plaque), or group a collection of glass, china, pottery, paperweights or whatever takes your fancy on a shelf round an attractive lamp with a patterned base or shade. Don't underestimate the pattern value of flower arrangements or house plants either – these can all add interest to a scheme. Suggestions for first aid for dull schemes are given on page 79.

How to co-ordinate pattern with pattern

The word co-ordinate has crept into the language of interior decorating over the last few years, and has already appeared quite frequently in this book, but what exactly does it mean when related to colour and furnishing schemes? The word was first used to describe a style of dress, when the manufacturers of separates (blouses, jerseys, skirts, trousers, cardigans, jackets, and so on) suddenly realised that we did not have time to tramp round the shops finding separate items that matched, so they started producing mix-and-match ranges where some garments were patterned and others were plain, but in which the colours blended.

It took the furniture and allied home industries only a short while to catch up with this trend, and the word co-ordinate applied to the home can mean a variety of things. For example, it can mean a matching fabric and wallcovering, although they rarely completely match because they are printed on different basic materials, and most manufacturers prefer the words 'companion fabrics and wallcoverings'. It can also mean exactly what it says: co-ordinated fabrics and wallcoverings, or designs that are co-ordinated within a separate fabric or wallcovering range. Here the pattern can be exactly the same but on a different scale; or one can be positive and the other negative; or one can be the reverse or the mirror image.

Sometimes a fabric or wallcovering is printed with a fairly bold design, and the co-ordinate has a repeat of part of the design – usually the background – or an individual motif repeated. One very pretty co-ordinated chintz range, for example, has a trellis effect printed on paper and fabric in several colourways on a white ground, with a companion paper and fabric that include the trellis background but incorporate flowers as well. If you were using this in a bedroom you might use the bolder paper with flowers on the bedhead wall, with the simpler trellis design on the others. The bedcover could have a panel down the centre made with the floral trellis, with the border and valance in the simpler design, and the window treatment could well be curtains in the full floral effect over a roller blind in the plain trellis. A living room scheme based on these co-ordinated patterns is shown on page 38.

Several ranges of soft furnishings have the same design printed on two different weights of fabric – one suitable for curtains and the other for loose covers and upholstery – and in some cases the designs are also printed in different scales and repeated on a wallpaper. If you were using this type of design for a country-style living room scheme, you might use the paper on one wall, paint the other walls to tone, have plain curtains over a roller blind patterned on the same scale as the paper, with loose covers in the larger scale and heavier weight fabric. Scatter cushions could be made in the curtain fabric, patterned and plain.

Some wallpaper ranges have companion papers which can be cut and used as a frieze on a plain wall to link with patterned walls, or which can be incorporated into a scheme with all the walls papered with the overall design and trimmed with the frieze at picture rail or cornice level. This type of decorative treatment is ideal for long living/dining rooms which may well have an archway or doors dividing them, but which should be treated visually as one area to give a feeling of continuity and greater space. In a room of this sort you could use a bold design on one of the long walls common to both areas of the room and a smaller companion design on all the others. Alternatively, you could paper the dining area with the patterned paper, paint the walls of the sitting area (which you want to be more restful), and then emphasise the archway with a strip of the border paper. You could also use the border paper as a frieze round the walls of the sitting area, or if it is a large room and the design is fairly bold, use it as a dado parallel to the skirting and about 1m from the floor. When one paper is printed with a large pattern and another with a small complementary design, cut strips from the smaller pattern and use it to frame the main one by running it as a border all round the edges of each wall flank. A number of ranges have three different designs that all go together, so it is possible to work out different permutations; these can also be used to co-ordinate designs from room to room and out into the hall, stairs and landing area – a scheme that always helps to make a small house appear much larger.

In a terrace house, for example, you might use a small pattern on all the walls in the dining room, a companion textured or striped paper on all the walls in the living room, and in the hall have the bolder co-ordinated paper on the wall at the side of the stairs, with the same paper as in the living room on the other downstairs walls, and the dining room paper on the landing.

It is very important to try and think of a house as a whole, and if you don't like the idea of using co-ordinated ranges, and perhaps prefer fairly plain interestingly textured surfaces, then at least try to plan the floorcoverings so that you do not get a terrible clash of colour and design from one room to another. You can buy patterned or textured-effect carpets that have matching plain ones, so here a good treatment might be to use a pattern in the hall and dining room, a plain carpet in the living room to tone with one of the colours in the patterned carpet, and different plain carpets in each of the bedrooms. In houses where there is a bathroom en suite with the main bedroom, these two should be treated decoratively as one room, even if you use a range of co-ordinates; you could paper the bathroom walls in a mini-print, use the bolder companion paper on the bedroom walls and the mini-print possibly on the ceiling, with window treatments in the different scales to blend. Co-ordinated ranges of bedroom and bathroom linens also exist and frequently include ready-made curtains, and these can be successfully used with plain walls.

These suggestions apply primarily to those designs which are intended to go together, but it is possible to mix floral patterns or geometric designs cleverly to create a similar effect even if they do not belong to a co-ordinated range, as you can see on page 44.

SANDERSON

STOREY BROTHERS

These four photographs illustrate various ways of mixing different patterns to good effect.
Above left: In this living room, the basic trellis design from a co-ordinated range is printed on wallcovering and curtain fabric, with the companion floral trellis fabric used for a roller blind.
Below left: Two different floral patterns have been combined successfully in this attic bedroom, a bold traditional wallcovering and a mini-printed fabric used for curtains and bedlinen.
Right: Bold diagonal-striped curtains in navy blue on white echo the butcher's apron design on the sofa.
Far right: This imposing four-poster bed has been hung with two companion fabrics, and the far wall is papered to match the inner curtains. The bedroom chair is covered in a related fabric, and patchwork cushions provide a link.

How to improve room proportions with pattern

As there are over twenty million homes in Great Britain alone, there are bound to be many rooms that are badly proportioned or have certain irregularities (which can sometimes add to their charm), but do not despair if you have an awkwardly shaped room – you should be able to spot the mistakes and disguise them with the clever use of colour and pattern.

Try to take a detached view of the room you are planning to decorate and furnish: consider its size and shape and decide on the atmosphere you want to create and the range of colours you want to use. Then ask yourself:

Is the room too tall, or possibly too long and narrow?

If it has sloping ceilings, are these attractive or do they make the room very dark?

Is the room wide enough in proportion to its height?

Is it square, box like and uninteresting? Does it lack a focal point?

Where are the windows situated: are they perhaps too large, or are they small and awkwardly placed? Do they let in enough light?

Are there any particularly ugly features, such as an overpowering fireplace, ill sited chimney breast, large ugly radiators or long runs of unsightly pipework?

Does the room have too many doors or windows, and do they seem to cut up the wall area?

Do you feel claustrophobic when sitting in the room, or lost in a vast sea of space?

All these problems can be dealt with and many of the faults corrected, but in trying to disguise the proportions and improve the atmosphere of a room it is important not to lose sight of its original function. A beautifully elegant kitchen, for example, is quite impractical if you cannot prepare and wash up meals easily, or if the surfaces are difficult to clean. A dramatically decorated bedroom will not be very functional if you find the decor too stimulating to get a good night's sleep, or if you don't have enough storage space for your clothes and are reduced to hanging them round the picture rail. Similarly a living room that incorporates all the items necessary for streamlined efficiency will not necessarily feel comfortable nor will it be an easy room in which to relax.

As I mentioned in the last section, colour is the most important single

The drawings on these pages show ways of using colour and pattern to alter the apparent proportions of a room.

1 Using stronger colour on the lower part of the walls (perhaps from the picture rail down, as shown here) makes a room look wider by reducing its apparent height. Reversing the process would have the same effect.

2 Another way of making a room appear wider is to use a flooring with a definite linear pattern running across the room. The ceiling should be painted to tone with the floor to draw attention to the pale side and rear walls, giving an impression of increased width.

3 Here the room has been made to look narrow and deep by using a strong horizontal pattern running from front to back on the floor and both side walls.

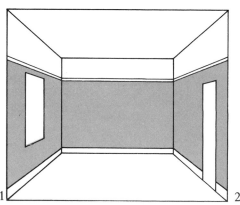

1

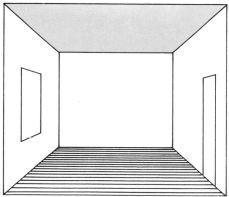

2

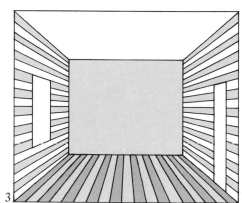

3

You can also play decorating tricks to make the floor area appear larger or smaller, as shown in the drawings below.
4 Here the floor area has been made to look smaller by laying a bright carpet square over a darker wall-to-wall flooring, leaving a generous margin.
5 A fitted carpet makes any area look larger, and this effect can be increased by painting the skirting board to match. If the same colour is also used on the walls, the whole room will look more spacious.
6 By laying tiles (or using a square-patterned floorcovering) diagonally, the eye is drawn from corner to corner – the longest dimension across the room – so making the floor area look larger. Light and dark floor tiles laid chequerboard fashion would create a similar effect.

factor in creating atmosphere, and it is perfectly possible to make a small, crowded room appear more spacious by using colour cleverly (see page 15), or conversely, to make a large barn-like area, such as a Victorian entrance hall, landing and staircase look warm and welcoming, but what other eye-deceiving tricks can you play?

If there is a very high ceiling, it can be made to look lower if you paint it a dark colour, picking out any ceiling mouldings, cornices or covings in white (you can put up pre-formed coving if there isn't one). It also helps to have a dark flooring in a similar colour, as the two dark areas appear to meet each other, thereby shortening the apparent height of the walls. Choose a wallcovering with a definite horizontal pattern, or in a room with large windows have a horizontal pattern on the curtain fabric, contrasting with plain walls, floor and ceiling in different strong colours to make it appear less lofty.

Often in Victorian and Edwardian properties the ceilings are high but the rooms are nevertheless beautifully proportioned, and if this is the case it is a pity to spoil the shape by trying to play decorating tricks. If the fireplace and overmantle have been removed, and the furniture is modern and low,

the room can seem overpoweringly tall, so try to correct this by having furniture of different heights; building sets of tall shelves into any recesses; and making a focal point of one wall with an eye-catching arrangement of pictures, prints and other objects massed together in a group.

Friezes or painted wall patterns can be used very effectively in tall rooms; use a frieze parallel to the cornice or picture rail, and again parallel to the skirting board, combined with a companion wallcovering or plain painted walls. Wall patterns can be painted in bold horizontal stripes and curves for a similar effect.

If the room is narrow as well as high, try to increase its apparent length by treating one of the narrow walls differently from the other three: you could use mirror glass or tiles; a mural, or a boldly patterned wallcovering; or paint it in a bold, rich colour with the other walls much paler. Alternatively make a definite horizontal feature of the lower part of the wall, again using the frieze technique, or make a dado by using a heavily embossed textured wallcovering, a patterned paper or horizontal wood cladding.

One way of dealing with a long narrow room, particularly when

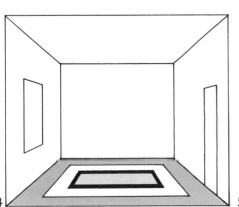

4

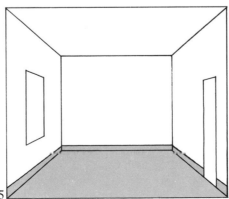

5

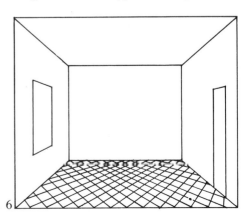

6

there are windows at each end, is to keep the walls fairly pale and plain and to make curtains from fabric with a bold horizontal pattern on it. Hang the curtains from floor to ceiling and wall to wall. If the windows are at one end only you could use a fabric which has a companion paper (use this on the wall opposite the window) and create a similar effect. Floorcoverings which have a definite striped or geometric pattern on them can be laid widthways across a room; light and dark tiles can be laid chequerboard fashion, or in stripes, to make an area appear wider. In long narrow corridors, try to make a focal point at one end with a bold pattern (paper or paint), a mirror or mural, or even a little *trompe l'oeil* – paint a simulated window with a view seen through it if the wall is blank; if it contains a door you can decorate it with a painted pattern (non-artists can buy special door murals).

If your ceilings are very low, use stripes or a bold vertical pattern on all walls; if there is a picture rail, remove this and take the wallcovering up to the cornice or coving. Paint the ceiling a pale colour, or white, and keep the floorcovering fairly light and plain to create an illusion of greater space and height. If you live in an old cottage with low timbered ceilings, try to keep the beams as light as possible, using white or a pale paint between them, and paint the walls the same colour or a little darker. It is best to confine pattern to the curtains in this type of room. Use simple furniture and choose low pieces of uniform height, or units that have vertical emphasis like the type that is supported on darker 'ladders'.

If the ceiling slopes, it can be decorated to match the walls: a pretty country atmosphere can be created with an overall floral pattern or a tiny mini-print; the charming effect is

MICHAEL NICHOLSON/EWA

enhanced further if a companion fabric is used for curtains and bedcover. If a plainer scheme suits the function of the room better, then a triangular pattern painted on the sloping area of the ceiling, following the shape, can look very effective.

If the room is square and box like, begin by adding a coving if there is none, use a boldly patterned wall-covering on one wall – behind the bed, for example – or have a complete wall of patterned curtain fabric, or use a really interesting texture in a strong colour; keep the ceiling and the other walls plain and fairly light.

Ugly features such as radiators and pipes can be 'painted out' to match the background. A most attractive treatment for an area festooned with pipes is to paper walls and ceiling with a patterned paper which has a flowing design, preferably with leaves, flowers and branches. The pipes can then be painted to match the most dominant colour in the paper.

This box-like dining room is made to look taller by the bold use of heavily striped wallpaper. The modern prints repeat the vertical theme.

The apparent proportions of this high-ceilinged living room have been improved by a decorative frieze from Osborne & Little. The ceiling has been painted the same deep colour as the walls to make it appear lower.

How to use floral designs

Many floral patterns are pretty and are frequently associated with co-ordinated wallpaper and curtains in period bedrooms and attics with sloping ceilings; chintz and cretonne fabrics used for loose covers and curtains in country 'anyone for tennis?' drawing rooms; blooming all over traditional patterned carpets; but there are lots of other types including modern stylized flower heads repeated all over a surface, and abstract treatments.

How should you set about using florals for maximum effect? If you want a soft, pretty, feminine room, then this is the place to use the more romantic or Impressionistic, slightly misty designs. If you prefer the room to have an old-fashioned or period flavour, then look for the Victorian and *art nouveau* designs, or a floral pattern combined with Regency stripes. If you have a small room to decorate, then consider the tiny 'Granny' prints, but in a large room you could use a more full-blown design. If you prefer modern schemes, choose one of the abstract or stylised treatments available.

Flowers do not have to be confined to the bedroom or bathroom; a country-style kitchen, for example, can look very fresh with flowers blooming all over the walls, particularly if they are combined with wood-grain units, checked gingham curtains with frilled edges and self-coloured tie backs, and a warm-looking cork floor. Florals can also look pretty on living room walls, so long as they do not clash with the upholstery fabric. In a sun lounge or conservatory extension to a house, flowers on the curtains and on the cushions on cane furniture can appear to bring the garden indoors, even if there are no house plants around.

Floral patterns are not necessarily suitable for use only in the country but not in towns. Just as green paintwork on the exterior of a house in the country can look wrong and quarrel with the greenery in the garden, so can many florals look out of place in a living room or dining room with immediate access to a beautiful garden, as they detract from it. But in a small town house, dark flat or basement bedsitting room, cleverly chosen floral designs can create a wonderfully fresh atmosphere and give a feeling of light and space.

Mixing like with like
Working with co-ordinated designs has been discussed in detail earlier in this section, and how to mix pattern with plain, but how do you mix floral patterns when they are not specifically designed to go together? Well, it can be done, but the designs must be of similar type. For example, a small

mini-print on the walls and curtains would not blend particularly well with a bold traditional floral carpet. If you plan to use this type of design on the walls and at the windows, then contrast it with a plain carpet. If you want to use the boldly patterned traditional type of floral carpet, then a striped or silky-textured wallcovering would show it off to advantage with perhaps a restrained curtain fabric covered with Impressionistic flower heads, or a self-coloured lacy effect with flowers woven into the design. They must be similar in feeling and in colours which harmonise. Scale is very important: you can use two different-sized floral patterns together – even three if they are co-ordinated or have the same pattern printed on different fabrics and/or wallcoverings (see page 34) – but if you are trying to mix two unrelated floral patterns together, then they must be in proportion to the size of the surface on which they are used.

How to use geometric designs

With geometrics, the rule about scale does not apply in quite the same way, but again they must be similar in type if they are to settle together happily in a room. A small squared pattern on a carpet, for example, can be enhanced by a large square design repeated on the wallcovering or echoed in paint on the walls, so long as the room is large enough to take a bold design. In a smaller area the design should be neat and unobtrusive – possibly a simple abstract design on the carpet, with plain walls bordered with a similar pattern. A fabric printed with a regular curving design can be used for curtains and the pattern can be repeated in a slightly larger scale in the form of wall patterns, painted on one or more walls. Chequerboard-effect floors, created with tiles of one kind or another, look particularly well with a geometric wallcovering.

Geometric designs nearly always say 'modern' unless they are a traditional Greek-key type of pattern, and they definitely look better used in a sophisticated setting in a fairly modern property, preferably one where there is a lot of light from large windows. They can also look just right in a study-cum-bedsitting room or a child's room. Somehow geometric designs always create a slightly stark atmosphere, and are never cosy as floral designs can be; they are rarely very feminine, and most geometric designs are highly stimulating and are therefore not the ones to choose to create a restful scheme.

Subtle stripes and checks can form a link between different patterns of one type in a room, whether the emphasis is floral or geometric, but they cannot successfully form a link between the two different types of pattern, so generally speaking, floral and geometric patterns should not be used together.

Three bedrooms where the bedlinen is an integral part of the decorative scheme. The pattern mix gives each room a completely individual look.
Opposite page : The co-ordinated floral designs used on the bedlinen in this country bedroom are complemented by the diamond pattern on the wallpaper.
Above left : The geometric mini-print on the walls is not too overpowering in this small bedroom, and the border-printed matching duvet cover repeats the theme.

Plain dark sheets, pillows and paintwork supply a strong contrast.
Above right : The striking geometric wallcovering and bold black and white paintwork are teamed successfully with the classic check bedlinen.

HARDY AMIES FROM CROWN

DORMA (CV HOME FURNISHINGS)

How to create period atmosphere with pattern

Many people like to decorate at least part of their homes in a definite period style, whatever the age and style of the property, and this nostalgic trend is increasing in popularity. Jacobean, Tudor, Regency, Georgian, French Empire (particularly for bedrooms) are all high on the list of period 'pops' as can be seen from the ranges of reproduction furniture and

traditional-style carpets and furnishings that have been available for years and are now being made in even greater quantities. Victorian, Edwardian, *art nouveau, art deco*, 1920s Bauhaus and 1930s Odeon are also styles that are gaining in popularity (many of the genuine items are still obtainable and are not always prohibitively expensive); possibly the trend will soon be for Festival-of-Britain contemporary!

If you want to set about creating a traditional room scheme of this type

you will find that, apart from having at least two or three items of furniture in the correct style, you will need to choose your patterned surfaces very carefully, since it is mainly the type of design used that helps to give a room a particular period flavour; texture also plays a part (see page 54) and colour to a lesser degree.

It is also important to choose an upholstery fabric in a pattern (or texture) that suits the style of the furniture; delicate pieces with inlay or mouldings would be quite spoilt if they were upholstered in a strident pattern or really rough texture. For example, Sheraton or Hepplewhite dining chairs (real or reproduction) call for upholstered seats in Regency stripes or brocade in fairly light colours and with a silky finish, to offset the rich mahogany frame. If the chair is a Chippendale one with Chinese influence, then you might choose a fabric with an Oriental flavour, but

again it should have a traditional look. Massive furniture, on the other hand, looks silly upholstered or loose covered in fabric with a tiny floral pattern: a 1930s 'club' style suite, for example, can take a bold geometric design reminiscent of the period, or for a country house atmosphere it could be covered with a large floral chintz such as a William Morris design. Heavier Tudor-style furniture, usually made in dark oak, looks effective if it is upholstered in tapestry, figured velvet or even one of the heavy linen hunting prints.

To find out more about furnishing and decorating styles of the particular era that interests you, you can again visit stately homes, exhibitions and museums; pictures in art galleries can often supply a wealth of detail, but books and magazines are also helpful, and the local library should be able to assist with suitable reference material. If you are lucky enough to live in a mellow old house, then it is very satisfying to restore some of the rooms to their former glory, although it is not necessary to copy an interior slavishly – a little mix and match of style can add sparkle to a scheme. If you live in a very modern house with lots of interestingly textured walls and floors and very large windows, it is not always possible to create a very definite period atmosphere; in fact it is wise not to try, since the decorations could clash unfortunately with the architectural style of the building. It is better to introduce some interesting old pieces of furniture, ornaments, pictures or other accessories, placing them very carefully for maximum effect and illuminating them skilfully. Then they are shown off to great advantage by the interesting background and help to draw attention to their stark modern surroundings.

Some of the earliest styles of interior decoration did not incorporate much in the way of pattern. Cave men, of course, painted pictures on their walls, and so did the Etruscans; the Romans often relied on their mosaic pavements to provide design interest, although they did have wall paintings as well. In Northern Europe in the Middle Ages, tapestry hangings (used to keep out the draughts) were often the only patterns to be seen, against rough stone or brickwork with rush-strewn floors and basically simple furniture made from the most readily available wood, and with iron and pewter for accessories. Then the more luxurious velvets and brocades appeared for upholstery of simple chairs, as hangings for four-poster beds and eventually as window curtains. Carpets from the East and the Orient with their formal and very distinctive type of design introduced more pattern, and by the Regency era (1811) the fashionable Oriental influence was apparent in patterned lacquered furniture; exotic Chinese wallpaper and painted panels; and wrought iron was worked to look like bamboo. But nowadays if a 'Regency' scheme is required most people think of Regency striped wallcoverings and fabrics.

To create a Regency dining room, for example, you could choose items from the wide range of reproduction furniture available, preferably in mahogany; have the chairs upholstered in a gold-and-white Regency-striped brocade and use this same fabric for curtains, suspended from brass poles. Paint the walls and ceiling in Wedgwood blue, picking out any cornice and ceiling mouldings in white. If the room is box like, put up a pre-formed coving and ceiling mouldings if possible; these are readily available in fibrous plaster, gypsum and polystyrene. Paint them white to stand out against the blue background. If the room is large enough, make panels on the walls from beading and pick this out in white; inside the panels you could hang a paper with a definite Chinese look, or a gold flock wallcovering, or a gilt-and-white-striped paper. Ceiling panels could also be made using similar beading and coving. Complete the scheme with an Oriental rug in golds, blues and white on a polished wood floor. The Regency stripes and Oriental carpet will set the correct style.

If you want a traditional bedroom scheme, then the French 'boudoir' style could be the answer. Start with the carpet, which should be patterned, and might well be a copy of an Aubusson, but could equally well be a pretty floral with flowers and ribbons, in rose, greens, gold and off white. All fitted furniture should be painted off white and trimmed with gilt beading typical of the period (some units are sold with this beading on, but it is also possible to buy this type of trimming and fix it in place yourself). The bed could be a four poster with slim pillars in mahogany or off white and gilt. For curtains and bed drapes use a glazed chintz printed in rose and green on off white. Cover the walls with a silky-textured paper or vinyl wallcovering, or even use actual fabric, in either rose or soft green. Complete the scheme with touches of brass. The pattern on the carpet and soft furnishings will give the room the desired atmosphere and will look right with the furniture.

If your taste runs more to the 1930s you might decide to use as a bedhead a triple mirror with arched top from a dressing table of the period, with one or two pieces of 1930s furniture. Wall patterns in pinks could be painted on the bedhead wall, echoing the shape of the bedhead, to give the room that typical 'Odeon' look. The other walls could be papered with a black and white design showing fashions of the 1930s, or one printed in pinks and grey on white with the popular cloud effect of the period. The carpet should be luxurious with a long pile and curtains might well be pink satin.

In a late Victorian or Edwardian house you may well decide to use the *art nouveau* designs popular at the turn of the century, and which were originally produced by William Morris, Voysey, Vigers and the other followers of the Arts and Crafts Movement. Many of their lovely flowing floral designs are still being printed today on fabrics and wallcoverings, although some have been scaled down to suit today's smaller rooms. An *art nouveau* style living room would be an ideal place to use co-ordinated wallpaper and fabrics (see page 34). All the walls could be papered with a slightly scaled-down version of William Morris's classic Golden Lily design in soft green, gold, apricot and orange, with ceiling and woodwork picked out in off white. The companion fabric, in a larger scale on a linen/cotton union fabric, could

be used for covers on a Chesterfield sofa, with chairs covered in a plain burnt-orange linen with loose cushions in the smaller-scale design printed on curtain fabric. Floor-to-ceiling curtains in a natural hessian trimmed with burnt orange could hang over a neat sill-length roller blind made from the small-scale curtain fabric. The scheme could be completed with a cord or sisal carpet in soft green, with *art nouveau* accessories – it is still possible to find examples of the decorated glass, silverware and china of the period. Stained-glass panels used decoratively would also be in keeping: they might be fixed to the window so that the light filters through, or stood on the ledge; or if displayed in an alcove or recess they could be lit from behind.

Talking about texture

The skilful blending of different textures in a room is just as important to the success of the scheme as the choice of colours and the mixing and matching of patterned and plain surfaces, yet it is often a neglected subject: textures are all too often put together in a most haphazard way even when the rest of the scheme has been carefully balanced. The selecting of textures needs even more care and attention when a room is being decorated with mostly plain colours on the larger areas of walls, floor, windows and on upholstered furniture. If all these surfaces are of the same texture, even if the colours are different, the final effect will be boring. Just as a successful scheme in mainly warm or cool colours needs a sharp contrast from the opposite side of the colour wheel to bring it to life, so textures need contrast for emphasis.

Textured surfaces give not only visual, but also tactile satisfaction. Think of rough, smooth, shiny or matt surfaces: the comforting feel of an exposed brick wall; the homely warmth of tongued-and-grooved wood cladding; the harsh clatter underfoot of marble or ceramic flooring; the opulence of satin curtains; the polished perfection of mirror glass; the enveloping richness of velvet or plush upholstery; the luxury of leather; the natural look of hessian wallcovering. But texture can be ethereal too: a pattern formed by sunlight filtering through a coloured glass window, or through a Venetian blind; the fragile cobweb effect of open-weave curtains; the frothy foam of lace; the filigree tracery of wrought iron and canework.

Texture is also definitely linked with colour, and colour is affected by texture. On a flat surface some colours appear dull, but on an interesting textured surface the same colour can look alive and interesting. Smooth surfaces reflect light and dull ones absorb it, so the same colour may look lighter, for example, in an emulsion paint on a wall than it would in a tweed or velvet upholstery fabric or on a silky brocade curtain material. Even two carpets dyed with the same pigments can look different if one has a smooth velvet pile and the other a looped, nubbly weave or a long shaggy pile. When a scheme is being built up based on the different versions of one colour, it is essential to use contrasting textures to avoid a dull effect.

A dark, highly polished surface reflects the colour and shape of its surroundings: a rich mahogany dining table, for instance, can become almost a mirror of the room. A reflective surface, such as mirror tiles or highly polished ceramic tiles, if used on part of the wall area can improve the room's proportions or make a dark area appear lighter. Conversely a dark, matt surface will absorb the light and make large rooms seem smaller and more intimate; if all four walls, the floor and the curtains in a small room have a matt texture, the room will appear to be even smaller.

A very light, or white, matt surface both reflects and diffuses light and consequently enhances both natural and artificial light. This would be a wise choice for the walls of a small room that lacks light, or when a feeling of spaciousness is required. However, some introduction of silky and shiny textures would be essential in such a scheme, and in a small modern living room, for example, wall-mounted unit furniture in white plastics laminate;

The clever combination of different textures in this modern living room creates a sophisticated, restful effect, and the strong sunlight pouring in emphasises the variety of finishes. The shaggy woollen carpet introduces a soft contrast to the hard brick, wood and metal surfaces.

51

chrome and smoked glass coffee tables;
a large mirror (or area of mirror tiles)
and leather upholstery could
effectively be added to a scheme with
matt white walls and ceiling, shiny
white woodwork, polished wood floor
with rugs and woven tweed curtains.

It is vitally important to achieve
a successful balance between the
different types of texture used in a
room: they need to be mixed as
cleverly as patterned and plain
surfaces; there should be enough
contrast to make the scheme
interesting, and yet they should not
'scream' at each other. Of course it is
unlikely that a room will consist
entirely of plain, textured surfaces,
because some textures appear to be
patterned. In our neutral-coloured
and luxuriously textured room setting
shown on pages 5 and 79 the carpet
is woven from different versions of one
colour, and the effect is rather like
ripples on a lake – mainly texture, but
there is a slight element of design.
The vertical window blinds have an
interesting textured surface, and the
combination of colours on the
upholstery creates a subtle effect.

If you have used lots of pattern in a
room, you will still need some contrast
of texture on the various surfaces.
Imagine you are planning a very
feminine bedroom in a country house,
based on a rose-pink sculptured pile
carpet, and the walls are to be papered
with a floral pattern, which is to be
echoed on dainty cotton curtains. You
may well decide to have semi-sheer
curtains with a woven self-coloured
floral pattern to echo the design on the
cotton curtains, but the textures of the
main surfaces would be totally
different. A patchwork or crocheted
lace bedcover would be in keeping
with the style of the room, yet would
provide more contrast, and the scheme
could be completed with a mirror in a
gilt frame and some brass lamps.

Texture sets the style

If you want to create a certain period flavour or modern atmosphere in a room, pattern helps enormously to set the right theme (see page 46), but the choice of textures is equally important. Certain textures seem absolutely right in a traditional setting, yet would be out of place in a modern room, while others would enhance a contemporary room and yet do nothing for a period scheme. You need to 'feel' your way to the correct type and balance of texture.

Somehow brass, for example, complements a Victorian, Edwardian, Georgian and Regency scheme, but would usually look out of place in a traditional Tudor setting, except possibly for horse brasses on the beams or in an inglenook fireplace. You could create a Victorian-style living room, with upholstered seating in leather and plush; a rich-looking flock wallcovering; velvet curtains over heavy crocheted lace blinds; a dark Turkey carpet on stripped and sealed floorboards; and an elegant mixture of beautifully polished mahogany furniture and some delicate cane items. In this scheme textural contrast could be added in the accessories; the curtains could be suspended from brass poles with brass rings; some of the lighting might be by converted oil or gas lamps with brass bases and etched glass shades; wax fruit or flowers under a glass dome could stand on a circular table with a floor-length chenille 'skirt'; a cane what-not would be an ideal place to display a collection of Victorian knick-knacks. The shiny and slightly harsh textures of most of the accessories will set off the richer, softer feel of the chenille, velvet, plush and flock yet still be in keeping with the period.

If you prefer a Jacobean-style room, where the furniture, woodwork and doors are likely to be heavy and dark,

PETER BAISTOW

A gleam of brass adds a traditional touch to this room. The large mirror doubles this effect and gives the impression of increased space.

the accessories and accents could include velvet, silk, black wrought iron and an occasional gleam of pewter. Adding accessories in this way can often save a dull scheme, and the section on accents and accessories (page 73) tells you more about this.

A modern living room setting would combine a different range of textures again: possibly one wall would be finished in exposed brick or stone, two others in wood cladding and the fourth in hessian; the window treatment could be curtains in an open-weave sheer fabric over a Venetian or roller blind; furniture in chrome and smoked glass with other items in white plastics laminate finish; upholstery in canvas,

leather and nubbly tweed; flooring a practical tiled surface or sheet vinyl. Such a room would need the softening influence of shaggy-pile Rya rugs; a large terracotta crock filled with dried grasses, flower heads and leaves in neutral colours, or a varied collection of green house plants; some cushions in printed linen and crocheted wool and pottery lamp bases with silky slub-weave shades.

The textures used in a modern bedroom would need to be more stark than a traditional or 1930s one, but not so harsh as the suggestions for the living room. To set the right style you might cover the walls with a hessian-textured vinyl wallcovering; paint the ceiling and woodwork matt white; choose a Berber-type carpet and hang a striped linen-weave fabric at the window. This scheme would look well with light pine furniture, perhaps with a bed base and a run of drawer and cupboard units along one wall. The finishing touches could include sheets, pillowcases and duvet cover in a dainty printed cotton mixture; a chair upholstered in heavy ribbed corduroy; metal lamp bases with crocheted fine string shades, and decorative coloured glass bottles on the dressing table.

A country-style kitchen may well be based on the warm look of wood, whether real or laminated, with the floor covered in terracotta quarry tiles or traditionally shaped Spanish, Italian or Portuguese ceramic tiles. This room would need checked gingham curtains with frilled edges and hems; a collection of house plants or herbs growing in pots or a window box; a dresser or shelves filled with pretty blue and white china; a little cane or basketwork and lamps in either copper or brass. Once you start using and mixing textures in this way it becomes easier to see, and you can feel your way to the correct style for your room scheme.

*Above: Rough-hewn stone walls contrast
with polished wood ceiling and banisters
in this living room conversion. The
soft furnishings and skin rug provide
a textural contrast.*
*Right: This dramatic living room scheme
is a good example of skilful mixing of
different textures. The whole range has
been used, from the hard brilliance of
mirror, chrome and glass through
natural wickerwork to the soft tweedy
carpet and slub-woven wallcovering and
vertical blind.*

How to use textures

Textures contribute to the atmosphere of a room, and they also help to set the style, but it is not always easy to decide exactly which ones to use and what to contrast with what. In fact, the basic principles of using texture are the same as for colour co-ordinating.

Smooth and shiny surfaces such as marble, alabaster, glass, mirror, stainless steel, chrome, brass, copper, pewter, silver, ceramic tiles, emulsion paint, gloss paint, plastics laminates, silk, satin and foils are all cold to the touch and consequently bring a cool atmosphere into the room in which they are used – just like the cooler colours in the colour wheel (see page 7). If you want to create a very spacious effect (particularly in a confined area) then this is the place to use some of these smooth and shiny textures, preferably in light colours. The really shiny, reflective surfaces such as mirror, glass, high-gloss paint, glazed ceramic tiles and metal, can create such an illusion of space that if they are cleverly used they may make a room appear to be twice its actual size. So this group of textures can be used to help play decorating 'tricks', just as pattern can be used to create optical illusions (see page 40).

Contrasting brick walls – three painted white, one left plain – wood clad ceiling, quarry tiled floor and simple furniture give this room a modern look. The harsh textures are softened by ribbed velvet upholstery, an oriental rug and masses of house plants.

TIMOTHY QUALLINGTON

These cool materials must be relieved by some contrasting warm ones from the rough or natural group, just as cool colours need a few hot accents to show them off to advantage. For example, a small bathroom can be made to look bigger if mirror tiles are used on one wall and the bath panel; the floor in highly glazed ceramic tiles; all other walls, woodwork and ceiling could be gloss painted; the warm addition of a long-looped cotton-pile rug, towelling curtains and some plants or an arrangement of dried flowers and grasses would be necessary. Similarly an elegant but rather austere living room with gilt and white satin-striped wallcovering, brilliant white gloss woodwork, leather upholstery, polished mahogany furniture, shiny velvet-pile carpet and a lot of brass accessories would need softening with coarse lace curtains or a blind under velvet, plush or chenille curtains; cushions in tapestry, slub-weave silk and patchwork; and some seasonal flower arrangements, alternating with dried flowers.

Rough, natural, non-reflective surfaces such as unpolished wood, cork, textured woven fabrics, looped and cut-pile carpets, sisal and rush matting, brick, stone, hessian, linen, grasscloth and heavily embossed wallcoverings such as Anaglypta, are all warm textures and, like the warm colours of the spectrum, they help to contribute to a cosy, intimate atmosphere. They can make a room appear smaller (and quieter) and will certainly give it a pleasing warmth and create an atmosphere that is easy and pleasant to live in but, like the previous group of textures, they need the contrast of some smooth, shiny materials to emphasize them. A study with three hessian-covered walls and the fourth covered with cork to make a giant-sized pinboard; sisal carpeting; nubbly tweed upholstery and sheer wool curtains could be livened up with a collection of prints with metal (chrome or steel) frames; a highly polished wooden desk and a metal and glass lamp.

Textures are affected by light, even more than colour and much more than pattern: shadow tends to darken colour and to make texture more obvious, so if you want to use a heavily textured wallcovering it will show up better next to the window than opposite it, just as a lovely textured fabric will look better *against* the light as curtains, rather than as the upholstery for furniture placed in front of the window. Any of the rough, natural textures such as brick, stone, wood and cork benefit from side lighting and appear to give off a warm glow, but a shiny gloss-painted or smooth emulsion-painted wall similarly lit would show up any imperfections. So if the plasterwork in a room is less than perfect, consider using a rough or natural textured surface to hide it, rather than a smooth or shiny one, which would show up the defects in the wall.

The three dimensions

Before you get down to decorating or start replanning a room and choosing colours for it, it is as well to remember that the three dimensions of the floor, the walls (and ceiling) and the windows are the really dominant surfaces. Consequently, a practical approach is essential when it comes to choosing a floorcovering; a suitable wall treatment: wallpaper, vinyl, fabric or paint; and how to dress the windows.

First of all decide on the function of the room, for no matter how attractive the colour scheme or beautiful the furniture and furnishings, if the room does not fulfil the function for which it is intended, you have a decorating failure on your hands. Think also about the needs of your family and your particular life-style. For example, if you have a lively family and several hair-shedding pets, a patterned, or at least heavily textured and easy-to-clean floorcovering is essential. Walls should be washable, so that sticky finger marks can easily be removed: this usually means paint or a vinyl wallcovering; and the curtain, loose cover and upholstery fabrics should be washable too. Colours can be rich and robust rather than fragile and pastel. On the other hand, if you are planning a scheme for the master bedroom in a bachelor flat or an adults-only living room, the carpet can be light coloured, possibly with a long shaggy pile. The walls might be papered with a delicate oriental or hand-blocked paper, or painted with matt emulsion in a light colour, and the furnishing fabrics could be of silk, velvet or brocade. (There is advice on suitable surfaces for different rooms on page 66.)

Opposite: The main surfaces of floor, walls and ceiling have been decorated in plain colours to act as a foil to the simple traditional furniture and well chosen accessories in this comfortable dining room.

Floorcoverings

Having decided on the practical aspects, which dimension should you start with? Well, as the floorcovering (particularly if you are thinking of an all-wool velvet-pile carpet) is likely to be a fairly expensive item, this is the most sensible starting point.

An expensive mistake can be a disaster which you may well have to live with for a long time. Having established the fact that rooms which get the most wear need the most hard-wearing floorcoverings, where do you go from there?

Much confusion exists about the different types of flooring and floorcovering available, particularly carpets, and there are also newer types of flooring which have been developed over the last few years such as thermoplastic and vinyl tiles; cushioned vinyls in sheet form; carpet tiles, as well as sisals and mattings. Also there is the return to popularity of wood-block flooring, cork tiles and ceramics, particularly now these compare very favourably in price per square metre with a good quality carpet – and are likely to last longer.

Bear in mind that if you opt for a patterned carpet, it is likely to look bolder and brighter when seen over a large expanse. Try to see as large a sample as possible – and on the horizontal plane, exactly as you will see it down on your floor. If you are not sure about the effect of a patterned carpet in your room (a bold design can make the room appear much smaller, but a plain one is definitely too impractical), you could compromise with a small, neat geometric design or a simple 'tweedy' texture.

The type of flooring required for each room varies greatly according to its function; suitable floorcoverings are dealt with room by room in the section which begins on page 66.

Wall treatments

Throughout this book you may have noticed the word 'wallcovering' crops up again and again, and are probably wondering exactly what it means, since up until fairly recently walls in most houses were either painted or papered. In the more stately homes, some may have been draped with fabric, panelled, or painted with a design to simulate a three-dimensional effect and give an illusion of greater opulence and space. Walls in the service areas of most homes were usually tiled, gloss painted or clad with a special long-lasting finish.

All this has changed and nowadays wallcoverings is the term used to embrace plain, printed wallpaper; heavily embossed papers like Lincrustas and Anaglyptas; vinyl wallcoverings which can simulate any number of different textures; foils; hessians and grasscloths; cork and wood claddings; special heavily embossed vinyls which look like tiles; thin metallic sheetings and tiles – the list could go on and on. And of course if you still prefer to paint your walls, then you can choose from a range of about ten or twelve different types and literally thousands of different colours.

In most rooms the walls are 'on view' more than any other large area, since the floor is normally partly obscured by biggish pieces of furniture, so you should choose your wall treatment carefully; on the other hand it is the easiest (and often cheapest) surface to change. Most wallpapers, unless they have a metallic effect, can be overpainted easily and with the various non-drip thixotropic (jelly) paints available, you can repaint a room with one or two coats in a weekend without even splashing the carpet! Some wallcoverings (particularly vinyls) are easy to strip and come away leaving a soft lining

paper for overpainting or repapering. And with ready-pasted papers and vinyls, which you simply cut to length, immerse in a trough of water and then hang, you can repaper a room just as quickly as repainting it – and often without moving a single piece of furniture.

Having looked at your room as objectively as possible and decided on a basic colour scheme; whether to have patterned or plain walls – which to some extent will be determined by the other large surfaces in the room; what type of texture to use; you will need to decide on the actual wall treatment.

If you prefer plain walls, then emulsion paint is one of the most practical ways to achieve this – and you can choose from a matt, silky or slightly shiny finish in a fantastically wide range of colours. If you want a really subtle scheme look for the type with 400 colours or more which are produced by a tinting system, and which are mixed for you by machine in the shop.

Some papers and vinyls are almost perfectly plain, although they are usually slightly textured or embossed, but when hung this is scarcely obvious unless the light catches them in a certain way. There are also some unorthodox methods of achieving plain papered walls: for example you can use ordinary brown wrapping paper which you stick on with wallpaper adhesive or you can use bookbinding cloth which has a slight linen look and is available in some very good colours. For a more permanent surface in a bathroom or kitchen, you can get plain or textured ceramic tiles.

It is possible to pattern a wall with paint. Conventional effects can be achieved by drawing a scene and then painting a mural or a *trompe l'oeil* (eye-cheating) effect, particularly when you want to create an illusion of space and decide to paint an attractive view. But it is also possible to create all sorts of wall patterns using contrasting or harmonising paints, as shown here.

Remember that dark, bright or very boldly patterned walls tend to make a room feel claustrophobic, so a small room may well look better decorated with plain walls or a small minipatterned paper in fairly quiet colours. On the other hand a large forbidding room (particularly a big, cold hall) can look positively cosy if vivid, rich colours and strong patterns are used. Again try to see fairly large samples of paper and paint and try to judge the effect over all the walls of the room, remembering that bold designs and strong colours look two, three or more times as vivid when magnified over a large expanse of wall.

You can quite easily decorate a wall with painted stripes as shown here. First paint the whole wall in white or a pale emulsion.
Measure the area of wall you want to decorate, mark it out to scale on squared paper, and then work out your design within this outline.
Using pencil or chalk, draw a feint grid on the wall, making sure it is true and square. A set square, straightedge, plumb line and spirit level will all help with accurate marking up. Transfer your design from the squared paper pattern to the wall, scaling it up carefully.

Apply masking tape firmly on each side of the first stripe and paint it in boldly, being careful not to overpaint the outside edges of the tape.
Once this stripe is quite dry, remove the tape and apply new strips for the second stripe. Repeat this process until your design is complete.
If you find this too tedious you can cheat by painting strips of paper and then sticking them onto the wall where required.
Once you have perfected the technique of wall painting simple designs, you can graduate to more complicated murals and landscapes using the same methods.

Window dressing

There are so many different ways of treating windows, the subject could fill a complete book. Take curtains, for example: apart from the obvious problem of whether to have patterned or plain ones, there is the question of selecting the right fabric. Always make sure you choose a furnishing fabric and not a dressmaking material, since this latter is not always sun proof.

Windows let in the light and the view and so perform a dual function, but you may well want to be able to see out without being seen, so window treatments often have to exist on two levels – screening the glass and performing a decorative function. If the room tends to be dark, try to cut out the light as little as possible and take curtains past the window frame so that they hang well clear of each side of the window to allow the maximum daylight into the room. Remember that curtains are usually seen as part of the decorative treatment of the wall and so can blend and co-ordinate with the wall area surrounding them, if you want the window to appear

Left: A feature has been made of this dining room window by the inspired use of plants, roller blinds and an unusual lace hanging.
Above: A plain blind decorated with a Samurai and oriental foliage adds the finishing touch to this Japanese setting. Designed and made by Blind Alley.

JOHN MILLER

ERIKA CRADDOCK

These unique blinds have been individually designed and made for each room by Janet Semmens of Blind Alley. Not only are they attractive to look at, they also add an extra dimension.
Right: The blinds at the pair of sash windows in this blue bathroom are painted to reproduce the view of the town square outside.
Below: An imaginary country vista is the theme of the three blinds at the windows and French doors.

ERIKA CRADDOCK

TIMOTHY QUALLINGTON

63

unobtrusive. If, on the other hand, the room is large and you want to 'cut up' the expanse of wall, or the windows (or views from them) are so spectacular that you want to draw the eye towards them, the curtains and/or blinds should contrast with the surrounding wall area. Pattern is usually highly successful when used for curtain fabric since it has a greater fluidity than on other more static surfaces.

There are so many sorts of window – some homes have a different type in almost every room – and although you may not have actual problem windows, it can be difficult to choose the correct curtain styling for them. One way to decide is to look at your window as objectively as possible, then make a sketch of it and try out various curtain styles on an overlay (tracing paper) placed over the top of the window drawing. You will find there are many helpful illustrated soft furnishing books available, and curtain track and heading tape manufacturers give away useful booklets.

Blinds are an alternative to curtains, but they can also be used in conjunction with them: in a room with a radiator under the window, for example, a roller blind can be pulled down to the sill and the full-length main curtains drawn to the edge of the radiator only. The blind can match the curtains or contrast with them.

Venetian blinds can be used in similar situations to roller blinds, but have the added advantage that they can be adjusted to diffuse the light. A fairly recent development is the vertical blind, made in interesting textures – slub and silky weaves, for example. These usually open at the centre like a pair of curtains, and are particularly effective on large patio windows – they can also be used as room dividers. This type of blind is not usually used in conjunction with curtains but instead of them.

Sizing up

When thinking about the three dimensions, this might well be the ideal time to make a scale plan of the room, so that you can really get down to the practical aspects of planning; see if your furniture will fit and make sure of any simple structural alterations, such as installing new lighting or the removal of a fireplace, *before* actually doing any decorating.

First make a floor plan, which is a fairly simple operation. Measure the room accurately at floor level using a wooden yardstick or steel tape (cloth tape measures tend to stretch with use) and make a note of all recesses and projections, such as alcoves and chimney breasts, width of doors and windows, and their exact position in the wall. Then you should think three-dimensionally and measure the height of the room, height of skirtings, picture rail, frieze, and so on; the height of the windows and distance of the sills from the floor; the height of doors and fireplaces; and the widths and height of any built-in furniture. Also note the position of power and light points.

Draw out the room to scale on a piece of squared paper, using a soft pencil so that mistakes are easy to rub out – it can all be inked in later. A convenient size to work to is to make one square (1cm) on your paper equal to 25cm of the room measurement, a scale of 1:25. Mark in the exact positions of doors (indicate which way they open), chimney breasts and recesses, windows and so on, and indicate the siting of fixtures, fittings, power and light points and switches.

You can also make a wall plan (or elevation) of all the walls, using a similar technique, and make the whole into an open-topped cube (or line the inside of a box with them) to help judge any special effects you may want

to create. This 'exploded' technique is particularly useful if you want to try out some special effects in miniature before working on the real room, or for working out the correct window treatments.

Once you have completed your scale plan it is a good idea to measure the items of furniture to be used in the room, and to draw them out in the same scale on another piece of paper or card. Colour them with solid colour, cut out the shapes and move them about on the floor plan to establish their position. You can think three-dimensionally with the wall plans as well; this technique is particularly helpful for judging whether certain items will go under window sills.

You will find planning far easier if you draw a floor plan and elevations of each room, as shown opposite. The floor plan (centre) indicates the shape and size of the room, including chimney breast and recesses, and the position of the door, window and furniture. The elevations round it provide more details of each wall: position and height of the door, window, fireplace, skirting board, picture rail, shelves and power points. With this information you can work out how much paint, wallpaper and curtain fabric you need, and plan the layout of the furniture.

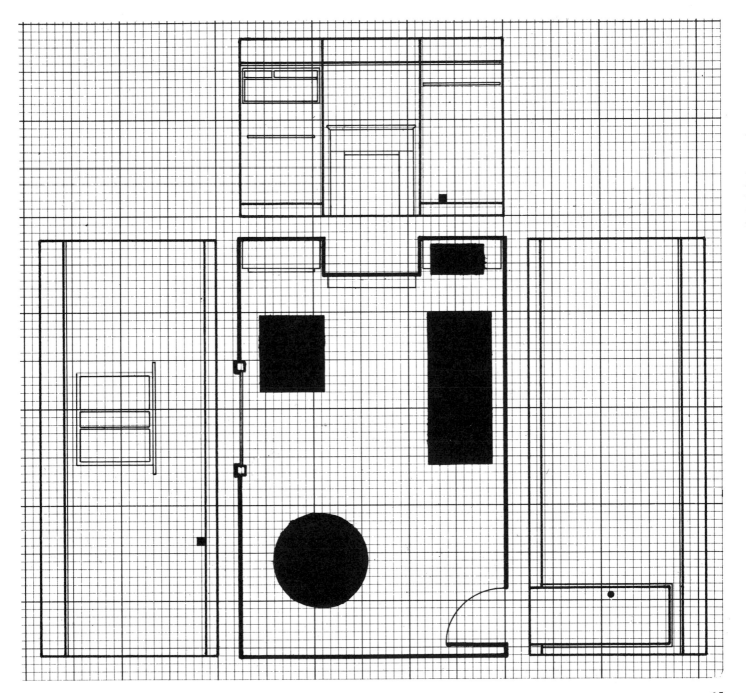

65

Live, eat, sleep

Homes are for living in: they are not meant to be beautifully decorated and then left untouched by human hand or foot! And *living* means that various activities have to go on in certain rooms: cooking and various domestic chores are coped with in the kitchen; the bathroom, apart from its usual functions, may also house a utility area and linen store; the dining room, dining area or kitchen are used for eating; the living room (or sitting room, lounge or drawing room – call it what you will) is normally a multi-purpose room, used for sitting and relaxing, entertaining, watching television, listening to music, and may have to provide a study corner as well; bedrooms are used mainly for sleeping, but often (as in the case of children's rooms) have to double as a playroom or later on a study. Halls are really the only area of the home that are not actually lived in – merely passed through, but of course they get a good deal of 'through traffic' in a house with a lively active family. It is therefore essential to be flexible in your approach to house planning, since you should be able to get maximum value from every room.

Whether the hall is large or small, as it is the first part of the home that visitors see, it should have a welcoming appearance. This does not necessarily involve great expense, however.
Above right: This spacious entrance hall has been given a simple monochromatic treatment in tones of gold yellow paint, with door panels picked out in white.
Right: Here the staircase in a small terrace house has been painted with cheerful yellow gloss paint.

Halls

When it comes to decorating the hall, stairs and landing, remember that this is the part of your home that is seen first by visitors and by the family returning home, so it should say 'welcome'; this calls for a warm, cheerful colour scheme, and if the house is a large one and the hall is vast, mix and match patterned and plain surfaces, and use dark rich colours to make it appear more cosy. Remember, when planning colour schemes for this

BERGER PAINTS

area, that since most of the other rooms lead off either the hall or a landing, it is vitally important to co-ordinate colour throughout, so you do not get unsightly clashes, particularly with the floorcoverings. If your home is fairly small, then you can link the schemes through from the hall and from room to room, with gentle colour changes, and create an illusion of greater space.

The hall, stairs and landing area is also one of the parts of the house which is subject to a great deal of wear and tear. Consequently wall surfaces must be practical and washable if possible. The flooring must be extremely hard wearing and easy to clean – one which does not show the dirt too much is a practical choice.

Kitchens and bathrooms

The kitchen and bathroom are the work centres of the house, and must be functional as well as practical – particularly the kitchen – and this means getting down to basic planning. If you are starting from scratch, as with children's rooms, choose furniture from a range that can be added to when the budget allows, and build up your perfect dream kitchen. Similarly, the bathroom usually has to be planned round the plumbing, and the size and shape of the room will determine the equipment you can or cannot have.

Both these rooms need practical decoration, but this does not necessarily mean they have to be clinical. Country-style kitchens are a pleasure to work in, particularly if they are in a town or suburban house: walls can be wood clad and sealed with a clear polyurethane finish, or you can use a fresh, floral wallcovering. If you prefer paint, choose a verdant country green or horizon blue; most kitchens are hot and sometimes steamy so cool colour schemes are particularly suitable, but if you have a cold, dark kitchen choose sunshine yellow, or mix apricot and orange. You can complete the pastoral effect with a pine dresser decked out with pretty china and copper, and if there is space a pine scrubbed table and ladder-back rush-seated chairs. Checked gingham curtains or café-style curtains would echo the country theme. Complete this scheme with sealed cork floor tiles, which are warm looking and practical.

Neutral colours and natural textures are also very successful in kitchens, with vivid splashes of colour which can be introduced in accessories and on curtains or a roller blind. It is essential to choose fairly plain, neutral worktops, since bright colours and strong patterns can be very difficult to live

These two kitchens illustrate how contrasting decorative treatments create totally different atmospheres.
Top: A cheap and cheerful paint job on inexpensive units gives the impression of a gypsy caravan.
Above: A fresh-looking room fitted out with crisp white units has bright green accessories for relief.

with and tiring on the eyes. The colour of unit door and drawer fronts should be chosen with care, too, as you are likely to have to live with them for a long time and will need to plan several different schemes round them. Favourite colours can always be introduced in accessories.

The same is true of bathroom suite and tile colours: the vivid fashion colours may be fun in an exhibition house or bathroom showroom, but think at least twice before you install them at home, since a bath, wash basin, shower, WC and bidet are very expensive to change and install. Some of the darker, trendy colours like aubergine, royal purple and even black are very tempting because it is possible to base a really dramatic scheme on them, but the 'high-tide mark' on a dark-coloured bath shows up as an unattractive grey scum and looks even worse than a black rim on a pastel coloured one! Coffee beige, golden green and butterscotch are easy colours to work with and lend themselves to several permutations.

Wall tiles can complement or contrast with the sanitaryware, but it is wise to avoid a very strong pattern; if you want a highly decorative bathroom, choose tiles in the same colour as the bathroom suite, or possibly veined with white, but only hang them as a splash-back round the bath and wash basin and to clad the walls of the shower. You can then use washable paper or a vinyl wallcovering on the area of wall above the tiles and ring the changes fairly frequently and at a fraction of the cost of retiling. Or you can pattern the walls with paint: one of the prettiest bathrooms I ever saw was painted to look like the fresh green countryside. An autumnal mural, showing trees in glowing golds, reds, rusts and browns, would look very effective with a gold or apricot coloured bath, particularly if the

theme was carried through into the floorcovering: this could be a carpet with a leaf design in autumn colours.

Flooring in both kitchen and bathroom is another important point to consider. In the kitchen it is essential that the floor is resilient and reasonably warm underfoot, but also that it is non slip, fairly waterproof and easy to clean. Ceramic and quarry tiles fulfil most of these requirements, but they can be rather harsh underfoot and tend to draw the feet, so consider something a little softer if you stand about in the kitchen a lot – sealed cork tiles are very attractive and resilient and can be cleaned with a damp mop. Cushioned vinyl, which comes in sheet form and in a wide range of different patterns and colours, is springy and very easy to lay and clean, and has almost replaced linoleum as a kitchen floorcovering. Vinyl and linoleum are both available in tile form. There are also special kitchen carpets made of compressed fibres, but frankly these are not really practical near the sink and cooker where they could get splashed with water, grease and other cooking spills; they can be used in the dining area of a kitchen, with a more permanent floorcovering in the cooking and food preparation area, as can carpet tiles.

Carpet tiles are also practical in bathrooms, since you can take up any which get saturated and dry them individually. Carpets which are made of synthetic fibres make better sense in a bathroom than all-wool pile. If the WC is in the bathroom and you have young children, carpet is not always practical; in this case choose one of the floorings suggested for the kitchen and soften it with washable rugs. Cotton looped pile ones are very attractive and come in a wide range of colours; this type of rug can also be specially ordered as a fully fitted carpet to cover the floor of your bathroom completely.

Living rooms

The two words to bear in mind when you are planning the furnishing and decoration of a living room are comfort and compromise. The furniture must be functional enough to fulfil the various family requirements, robust enough to take the occasional knock, *and* be comfortable to sit on or use. Since you don't want to be forever nagging the children to be careful, or banishing cats and dogs to other outposts of the home, surfaces must also be practical and easy to clean. You may fancy an off-white living room with a shaggy pile carpet; pearly painted walls and woodwork; oatmeal tweed upholstery; open-weave creamy wool curtains and fragile furniture; but this type of decor would only be practical in the grime-free atmosphere of a bachelor flat or an adults-only living room.

Begin by choosing a hard-wearing floorcovering; one which does not show the marks too much and one which can be washed or shampooed easily – or even taken up and changed round to even out the wear, such as carpet tiles or a carpet square. If you have very young children or are working to a low budget, it may be more sensible to use properly sealed cork tiles or do-it-yourself wood-block flooring (you can also strip, sand and seal good floorboards) softened with washable rugs. If you have decided to risk a plainish carpet, then it is worth considering placing a rug or two on top to protect the 'scuff points': usually the area in front of comfortable seating, under the dining table, or a 'traffic route' between two doors.

Washable wallcoverings such as vinyls and paint are the most practical finishes to choose, particularly if sticky finger marks are likely to be a problem; avoid too light a colour, although this will depend on the size, shape and aspect of the room. Upholstery should be as easy care as possible, and in reality this means selecting a fabric that is wipeable, if not completely washable, or loose covers which can easily be removed for dry cleaning. Curtain fabrics should be similarly easy to clean, or washable.

If the living room has to double as a dining room and there is no obvious divider, try to zone the areas with furniture, but without cluttering up the room too much. Different floorcoverings also help to separate the areas visually: the sitting area can be carpeted and the dining area have a more practical floorcovering such as vinyl or sealed cork.

Open-plan living was all the rage a few years ago, and some houses are still being built with the entire ground-floor living area – including the kitchen – open to view, and even the staircase rising from the sitting or dining area without let or hindrance. When it comes to choosing the colour scheme for such an arrangement, the whole area must be cleverly co-ordinated, and basically treated as one room, the stairs and landing area included.

If you add an extension to your living room, remember to make it harmonise: it should tone with the existing building materials from outside, but the inside colour schemes and decoration should blend as well.

Dining rooms

If the dining room is separate from the living room, and used mainly for family meals and entertaining, then it is possible to do some really exciting things with the decor, because it is not used all the time.

Surfaces have to be practical: a heat-proof top to the dining table, for example, or some sensible form of insulated cover-up. The dining chair seats, if they are upholstered, should be reasonably easy to clean, since food and drink are bound to be spilled occasionally, and the floorcovering needs to be easy to keep clean.

If you plan to have a carpet, choose one with a pattern (which need not be obtrusive) or a tone-on-tone or tweedy effect; if you prefer plain carpets, have a looped or twisted pile in a medium colour and in a fibre that is easy to clean. If the dining room is to be used for family meals and there are young children around, a washable or wipeable floorcovering such as vinyl tiles, sealed cork, linoleum or cushioned vinyl are worth considering, or loose-laid carpet tiles which you can take up and clean individually.

Dining room wall surfaces do not have to be quite so robust as in other rooms, but if you have a hatch through from the kitchen with a food serving area below, this wall should be easy to clean and not difficult to redecorate.

The style of decoration will depend entirely on your personal taste, the architectural bias of the property and your life-style. If you like a fairly traditional home, the dining room is often the ideal place to create a Regency decor as there are so many good pieces of Regency reproduction furniture available. The scheme can be based on a classical Regency-striped wallpaper or curtain fabric, or one of the lovely plain colours used by Adam: soft green, Wedgwood blue, terracotta or lilac, spiced with white. Country-style pine furniture or elm and beech chairs in traditional Windsor shape used with pretty fresh floral patterned wallcoverings and fabric can help to combine a timeless look with a modern interior, and a Jacobean room can be achieved with plain-painted, panel-effect or hessian-textured walls (or a wallcovering that simulates tapestry); rush matting or flagstone-effect vinyl floorcovering; printed linen curtains; 'planked' doors with heavy black iron latches and hinges; dark oak furniture and pewter accessories.

The mellow tones of the stripped pine furniture and the terracotta flooring give a warmth to this country dining room.

Bedrooms

The bedroom is one room that does not have to stand up to the rough and tumble of family life, so this is the room in which to use the more delicate colours, shaggy pile carpets, antique furniture, and fragile textures – if that is the type of scheme you want. On the other hand, bedrooms can be decorated in starkly modern style with basic furniture and the minimum of furnishings if that suits your taste, for this room can reflect the personality of its owner. In a double bedroom this may mean a compromise between 'his' and 'hers': the scheme should not be too feminine and frilly nor too masculine and severe.

The colours should be pale or subtle, and patterns should not be too bold; bright colours and strong designs are too stimulating for a bedroom, unless it is for a child (doubling as a playroom) or a teenage bedsitting room. If you want to use strong pattern, try to confine it to the bedhead wall (you don't see this when you are actually in bed) or to curtains and bedlinen; you can ring the changes with a variety of bedlinen designs, but remember to co-ordinate them with your bedroom colour scheme as they are seen without a becover when you are in bed. Try to have more than one bedcover as well, as this gives the room a different look: perhaps one matching the curtains, a dark one for winter and white for summer.

The bedroom is one place where the floorcovering can be chosen to suit your taste and pocket. If the bedroom is used only for sleeping, a carpet does not have to be particularly hard wearing or dirt resistant; indeed, if you long for an off-white shaggy-pile carpet, then this is the room in which to have it. In dual-purpose bedrooms the rules on living room floorcoverings are more likely to apply.

70

STOREY BROTHERS

Left: A traditionally pretty floral treatment for a girl's attic bedroom. The patterned wallcovering continues over the sloping ceiling, banded with stripes of paint. The soft furnishings are made up in a variety of related mini-prints.
Below left: Versatile shelving and a generous work surface provide a practical hobbies and study corner in this boy's bedroom.
Below: Most of the walls have been painted white in this children's playroom, as their own pin-ups provide adequate decoration. A washable cotton rug covers the hardwearing floorcovering.

BERGER PAINTS

JESSICA STRANG

Children's rooms

In most modern homes, a child's room has to serve as bedroom, playroom and study, so it must be practical and functional. The majority of surfaces should be easy to clean – fully washable whenever possible – and they should not show the dirt too much or you will be forever scrubbing or cleaning.

The most important thing to remember when planning rooms for children is that they grow surprisingly quickly. They soon outgrow nursery characters, so it is wise to use designs of the trendy type (depicting the latest television favourite, for example, if you can't avoid having them) only on surfaces that are easy to change; one wall or at most two can have a patterned wallcovering, but the others might be papered with an interesting texture which you can paint time and time again without having to strip the wall. Another practical place for design of this type is on a roller blind, which is only seen when pulled down at night – if the child later tires of the pattern on his blind you can add curtains; this 'double standard' insulates the room better and makes it darker at night in the summer.

Older children enjoy making their own wall of pattern and there are several ways of doing this: one is to make a collage wall from pictures cut out of books, comics and magazines, stuck in place with wallpaper adhesive; when the wall is complete it can be protected with a film of varnish or wallpaper sealer. This does make it harder to remove when you want to redecorate, but you can always reline the wall instead of stripping it. For a less permanent picture gallery, make a noticeboard wall: this can be covered with cork or cork tiles or you can use a fairly thick insulation board. Children also enjoy drawing on a large expanse, so to prevent them from scribbling on your walls, give them a blackboard.

Furniture for children's rooms should be chosen from a range of units or paintable whitewood to which you can add as the years go by, or could be basically simple pieces that will not quarrel with any items you may want to add later.

Apart from practical furniture and sensible wall treatments, the other important feature is the floor. When a child is small the flooring has to be washable which means buying either linoleum or vinyl in tile or sheet form, or using properly sealed cork tiles. Light and dark tiles laid chequerboard fashion are fun for floor games, hopscotch and so on, or the more adventurous can try designs inlaid in linoleum. Floorings of this type can be softened with rugs – the washable cotton type are the most practical.

Loose-laid carpet tiles may well be a practical alternative, as they can be taken up individually and cleaned – again two different colours look more interesting than a perfectly plain floor: they can be laid chequerboard fashion or to form an interesting border effect or outline a piece of furniture.

Adding accents and accessories

Once your room is decorated, the only thing that remains to be done is the addition of those little finishing touches which really bring the scheme to life and finally turn a house into a home. This does not mean every room has to be crammed full of bric-à-brac, for often the perfect finish to a scheme is provided by the lighting, but you may have to add that little extra-special something as well. Throughout this book, particularly in the section on colour (page 6), you will have noticed suggestions for completing a room with certain 'accents', in many cases introducing some sharp, contrasting colours to emphasise the colour scheme. These can often be provided by accessories, but you can achieve the same result in many ways.

You can paint recesses on each side of a fireplace to contrast with it, or hang a hessian or other textured wallcovering. A similar treatment can be used behind display shelves or to highlight a chimney breast. The contrasting colour can initially be introduced into the scheme in a patterned fabric, wallcovering or carpet where the main colours tone in with the scheme or are neutral – this accent colour can be echoed in certain accessories.

Since accessories can be as important to a room as wearing the correct shoes, hat, gloves and handbag is to a particular garment, you will need to choose those all-important furnishing finishing touches just as carefully as the original scheme. For example, gold shoes, bag and sparkling jewellery are suitable with evening dress but not with a daytime dress, and a large hat trimmed with flowers is often the correct accessory for a wedding or garden party but would look wrong with country-style tweeds.

To translate this dress sense into the home scene is not always easy. Although you can successfully mix and match different styles and periods in your accessories – some small antique pieces can help soften a stark modern room, and conversely one or two modern items will enhance a traditional decoration and furnishing scheme – you must be careful not to select things that 'scream' at each other or look out of place in the particular setting.

For example, brass and wrought iron fit well into traditional schemes, while chrome and stainless steel look better in 1930s or modern rooms; silk, velvet and satin cushions contrast well with a button-back leather sofa or printed linen loose covers; pleated chiffon lampshades can provide a delightfully feminine touch in a period-style bedroom, but a hessian texture on a pottery base would look better in a contemporary living room; pictures look well in most settings so long as their frames are chosen to complement the subject matter and not the room, but mirrors should be framed to suit the style of decoration.

In the living room

In living rooms accessories are often provided by scatter cushions; colourful book jackets; a collection of china, glass or pottery; some metalware such as silver candlesticks, pewter mugs, horse brasses, fender and fire irons or wrought-iron fittings; lamps and candles; pictures, prints, plaques, mirrors and wall hangings; butterflies, insects or a collection of fans, stamps, glove puppets, shells – all of which can be beautifully mounted in a box frame; table cloths (whether decorative or functional) and other table accoutrements; the list could go on and on.

When deciding on these accessories don't underestimate the effectiveness of simple things: a group of stones, or beach pebbles in unusual shapes and colours, can look enchanting in a modern setting, particularly if they are polished to a glassy perfection. An interestingly shaped bottle or jar, filled with shells or children's marbles and placed on a window sill or shelf where it catches the light, is an unusual accessory. Small stained- or painted-glass panels, different coloured glass bottles, or some decorative pieces of coloured glass can also look particularly effective in front of a window where the daylight will filter through them. Real fruit, artistically arranged in a basket or bowl, can provide an attractive and colourful centrepiece on a dining table or sideboard; there are some pretty wax, glass and china alternatives available, and all are fairly inexpensive. Fir cones, nuts, sun-dried maize and dried flowers can also be used to make interesting arrangements, and pieces of unusually shaped wood, bark or driftwood are well worth looking out for on woodland or beach walks.

Don't underestimate the effectiveness of indoor plants and flowers: they can often soften the harsh edges of a rather severe decorating scheme, particularly if you use prolific climbers and plants with variegated leaves. This sort of greenery is a fairly inexpensive way of adding green accents to decorating schemes, and there are so many different textures to choose from: fluffy and feathery; shiny and rigid; silky and ethereal.

Flower arrangements are less formal nowadays than they used to be, but in a traditional house with a natural niche or display shelves, or a large, important piece of furniture, there is still room for the more rigid type of floral display. Other flower

Traditional framed panels, an ornate gilded light fitting and carved chairbacks – all echoed by the flowing flower arrangement – create an atmosphere of art nouveau *elegance.*

ERIKA CRADDOCK

Far left: An amusing arrangement of china animals makes the most of this window plinth, flanked by two superb Victorian aspidistra pots.
Left: A dull view can be camouflaged, or a 'blind' window transformed, by the addition of glass shelves fitted into the embrasure for ornaments. Here a verdant effect is created by the use of an interesting variety of house plants.
Below left: Better than graffiti – a joke treatment for a small room. Walls, ceiling and pipes painted deep purple are a good foil for this collection of notices.
Below: This unusual group of seemingly unrelated objects is given cohesion by the clever choice of colour.

TIM STREET-PORTER/EWA

JESSICA STRANG

arrangements can be less elaborate: similar, colourful or self-coloured blooms grouped in a simple container; a collection of seasonal flowers; or a bunch of wild flowers; these all bring a pleasing personal touch to a room.

The important thing to remember when arranging accessories in a living area is not to space out one or two things sparsely: one eye-catching group is always infinitely better than a few isolated items. This is particularly true when hanging pictures, mirrors or other wall hangings – nothing looks worse than one or two hung dejectedly on the centre of each wall. Mass them together on one wall, preferably over a sofa, side table or sideboard or low unit, and never hang them too high: nothing should be above the eye level of the tallest member of the family. A word about safety here, too: never hang a mirror (or anything else that is likely to be looked at or into fairly frequently) above a fireplace, for even if the fire is adequately guarded, accidents can happen.

In bedrooms

The accessories in bedrooms can be similar to those in the living room, but they also include the bedcover and assorted bedlinen. Cushions are often neglected in bedrooms but can be grouped together very effectively on a bed or divan. Sheets, blankets, duvet or eiderdown cover are seen in relation to the entire room once the bedcover is taken off, so they should be chosen either to match or contrast with the colour scheme. There are so many co-ordinated ranges available that it is possible to select two or three different designs and/or colourways that will tone with the room and tone or co-ordinate with each other.

In the bathroom

The accents in a bathroom are usually provided by the linen; jars and bottles, soaps and bath salts; tissues and lavatory paper; towel rings, soap racks, mirrors, lavatory brushes and so on. The bathroom is also the ideal place to grow steam-loving plants (ferns or African violets, for example). There is no reason why bathrooms should not be accessorised with flower arrangements (real, dried or artificial), or used as a family portrait gallery or to display other pictures (so long as the atmosphere is not too steamy). If there is room, you can have towelling-covered floor cushions, or a big basket chair filled with smaller cushions. I have always thought the ideal accessory for a bathroom was the telephone, since it seems to ring particularly stridently the minute I lower myself into the water; it is possible to have one installed in the bathroom and there is now quite a good range of colours to choose from.

In the kitchen

In a kitchen the accessories have to be more practical and usually include china, pots and pans, plastic bowls, brushes, vegetable racks, pedal bins and so on. But again there is no reason why plants should not be grown successfully in the kitchen (but avoid the types that hate gas if you have a gas cooker or boiler), and it is the ideal place to grow a collection of herbs – possibly in a window box, where they will be handy for cooking. Strings of onions or garlic look very decorative, and so do baskets of eggs, and vegetables like aubergines, tomatoes and peppers are too pretty to hide away in a cupboard, so they can be put on display in attractive containers. Airtight glass jars can be filled with various different pastas, lentils, beans and other pulses which all look decorative as well as being cookable.

Lighting

Many rooms look wonderful in daylight, but the moment the curtains are drawn and the lights switched on at night the scheme can look dull and lifeless, because it is not properly lit. Lighting is one of the most important factors in decoration and one of the hardest things to get right, yet it is often left until last, although it should be thought about at room-planning stage, particularly if any structural work is likely to be involved. It is well worth reading the Design Centre book on lighting before you start to decorate; it is called *Planning Your Lighting* by Derek Phillips.

Lighting must be functional, particularly in rooms like the kitchen or bathroom, which are the work centres of the home, but it should never be harsh and should always contribute to the overall decoration scheme. Lighting has to be clear and strong where you want to prepare food, wash up, shave or make up, or where you want to sew, knit, read or study. Other vitally important areas for good lighting are the 'accident' areas of the home: the hall, stairs and landing; long, dark corridors; the front door; any understair (or other deep) cupboards; and the back door and sideway (particularly if you have to grope your way out to the dustbin).

Many lighting fittings may have to serve multiple purposes, and this is where dimmers are invaluable: a lamp in a living room, study corner or bedroom can easily be turned into a soft pool of background light when you don't need it to read or sew by. Central lighting fittings rarely have a place in the main living areas of a home these days, but downlighters (recessed spotlights) fitted into the ceiling at various points where good but unobtrusive light is needed work well in the kitchen, bathroom and hall.

Successful lighting like this contributes to and enhances the atmosphere in a room after dark.

Lighting is vitally important in a dining room, since you need to be able to see well enough to carve, serve and eat the food, but you may well want to change the atmosphere to suit the type of meal you are having: cheerful for family gatherings, more subtle for a dinner party.

Flexible background illumination could be provided by wall lights, individual lamps, spotlights or concealed pelmet lighting, but these should be separately controlled. Have a light over the dining table, preferably on a rise-and-fall fitting, which can be pulled up and down at will, with a dimmer control on it; this is ideal for lighting the table, but should never shine directly into the diners' eyes.

Curtains, if they are of a particularly beautiful texture or design, look much more interesting if they are softly illuminated at night; this can be done by concealing tubular fittings behind a pelmet (an ideal treatment for a tall landing window in a dark hall), so long as the fabric is not in danger of becoming over heated or scorched. Using spotlights is another practical way to light groups of pictures, display shelves, curtains and wall hangings. They can be mounted on electrified track which can hold several spots that can be beamed onto a particular object or in a particular direction; the track can be mounted on the ceiling, wall or on or under shelves.

It is essential to have as many lighting points as possible, so that you can have flexibility in your lighting scheme and to allow for possible repositioning of various pieces of furniture. Pools of light can then be provided by standard and table lamps, which are easy to move around the room. They should be decorative and in the correct style for the room, and the lampshades should balance the bases. Whenever possible, try a lampshade on the base before you buy it, and remember to see it lit and unlit – often the colour changes completely with the light filtering through, and the lamp and shade need to blend with the room scheme during the daytime as well as at night.

Light directed downwards towards the floor will make a tall ceiling appear lower, while light directed at the ceiling generally gives an illusion of height. To make a narrow room look wider, concentrate the light on the two narrow walls, leaving the longer walls in shadow. A collection of plants or flowers lit either from below or by a spotlight standing among them, can look really exotic: palms and rubber plants surrounded by other differently shaped, smaller plants, some with variegated leaves, light up particularly effectively. Ferns placed on a glass

table or shelf and lit from below can also look incredibly beautiful, and other objects on a glass shelf which is illuminated from below can appear to be suspended in space.

The few rules to remember when thinking about your lighting are: plan the lighting, particularly permanent lighting, *before* you start to decorate; light from above for clear illumination; light objects from the front if you want to emphasise them; let light flow across an object from the side to bring out details of shape and texture and to add drama; if you want to separate an object from its background, light it from behind to produce a halo effect; light things from below to draw them away from their surroundings.

Two views of the same room, by day (below left), and transformed at night (below) by subtle lighting and the addition of a well chosen table setting.

MICHAEL NICHOLSON/EWA

First aid for dull schemes

Sometimes even the most carefully planned scheme does not look quite as you expected once the room is finally decorated and furnished. What can you do to improve the situation? Well, it may not be all that dull – you could be too close to it, having worked on the scheme for so long – so ask the friendly advice of a member of the family or a sympathetic neighbour. If you are still disappointed with the results, take a long critical look at the room and see what you can do to improve it. Try adding accents and accessories as suggested on page 73, or look at the lighting and see if that can be improved (see page 77). If neither of these tactics works, try one of the first-aid suggestions given here before you do anything as drastic as redecorating.

The furniture could be wrongly positioned, but before you start humping heavy pieces round the room, try making a floor plan (if you haven't already done so) as described on page 64; size up the furniture in the same scale, cut out the shapes and move them around on the plan.

Sometimes a room looks dull because the furniture is too clinical – usually when it is mainly white with a laminated finish or mostly units in a very stark design – and the addition of one or two pieces in a warm-coloured wood can often save the situation. If the upholstery is all rather plain, a patterned or interestingly textured loose cover on one chair, or the introduction of a new piece of upholstered furniture in a contrasting fabric might help.

One of the most frequent causes of a dull scheme, in fact, is the use of too many plain surfaces in a room without the introduction of sufficient textural interest. You may be able to rectify this by making a group of varied cushions – some in plain fabric, others

Top: Ink-blue cushions and a dramatic hand-woven wall hanging by Elda Abramson add cool accents to this basically cool scheme.
Above: These two versions of our third room scheme (see page 5) demonstrate how the addition of contrasting accents can be used to bring a room to life. In the original scheme (left) the subtle use of neutral colours relies on the contrasting textures to create interest. However, this treatment lacks impact, so we added turquoise cushions and accessories. The result (right) is a well balanced monochromatic scheme with interesting accents.

79

patterned, and some in patchwork, a few could be embroidered or have a tapestry effect; placed on plainish upholstery or bedcover they can make the room look much more interesting. If this type of scatter cushion is not practical, then two or three contrasting floor cushions might be the answer.

If you want to bring the pattern or textural interest into the room on one wall only, then you could hang a patterned or textured wallcovering on one wall or in alcoves, recesses or possibly on a projecting wall like a chimney breast. This should link with the colour scheme, but might also introduce an accent colour and be combined with a neutral such as white. Murals, if they are appropriate to the general style of decor, can also help in this situation. Sometimes a plain splash of a bright colour is all that is needed, and again an area of wall might be painted or papered to contrast with the main scheme. A cork or other noticeboard for a changing scene of pin-ups could add interest to a child's room or teenage bedsitting room, or could be a practical addition to the kitchen or hall.

There are other ways of making a wall area appear to be patterned without actually resorting to new decorations: a group of different-sized pictures, wall hangings and mirrors almost covering an entire wall can suddenly make it look much more interesting.

Plain walls can be treated to look as though they are panelled by pinning up picture-frame beading to form false panels; you can then hang a patterned or a textured wallcovering inside them, or paint the area to contrast or tone with the surrounding wall colour. A rug hung on the wall, whether it be an expensive Oriental one, a cheap Indian Numdah or even a printed blanket, will immediately bring pattern, texture and new interest into the scheme. An attractive piece of patterned fabric can also be used as a wall hanging.

If the carpet or other floorcovering is plain and looks dull, then a patterned or heavily textured rug placed in front of a sofa in a main sitting area; at the bottom or side of a bed; or in the hall or on a landing; can break the plain area visually, making it seem smaller and more intimate.

You should not have to resort to using first aid too often if you plan things properly. The important thing to remember, whichever room you are about to decorate, plan or furnish, is that it should be practical and functional, serving the purpose you (and your family) require. At the same time it ought to be comfortable and easy to live in – and this means easy on the eye as well. All the rooms in your home should have the unmistakable stamp of your personality on them; at the same time each one should have the specific atmosphere you want, whether this be elegant and spacious, cool and clinical or intimate and cosy.

I hope that, having read this book and looked at the pictures, you will be inspired to try your hand at colour scheming, mixing patterned and plain surfaces together, experimenting with contrasting textures and creating some unusual and attractive interior decorating schemes. Don't be overawed by the theory, go round with your eyes (and mind) receptively wide open and, above all, *enjoy* putting your ideas into practice. Over to you – and have fun!

Further help

Many of the women's magazines offer advice on decoration and colour scheming, among them *Good Housekeeping, Homes and Gardens, Ideal Home* and *Pins & Needles*. Charges for these services vary according to the magazine.

Many of the major paint and wallcovering companies run colour scheme advisory services; some of them charge a small fee.

Berger Paints operate The Berger Colour Scheme Service, and you can write to them for details and a form at: Berger House, Berkeley Square, London W1X 6NB.

Crown Decorative Products have a comprehensive decorative advisory bureau; they have regional technical advisory offices and studios, but in the first instance you can contact them at the head office: Crown House, PO Box 37, Darwen, Lancashire BB3 0BG. They also advise on colour by post.

ICI will give colour scheme advice if you contact the Paints Division at Wexham Road, Slough SL2 5DS. Their booklet 'Getting it Together with Vymura' is very helpful; send for a copy to: Consumer Services Department, VGT, address as above.

They have also recently introduced Dulux Colour Centres, where you can look at a variety of colour-scheming aids. Advice on individual schemes will also be sent by post for a small fee. Write for more information to John Martin, Dulux Colour Centre Information Bureau, 84 Baker Street, London W1M 1DL.

Nairn Coated Products operate the Kingfisher Interior Design Service. You can write to them for a form and details at: Lune Mills, Lancaster.

Sandersons offer help in the advisory studio on the second floor of their showroom at 52 Berners Street, London W1A 2JB.

Further reading

Book of Home Improvements
Reader's Digest Association, 1976

Collin's Do-It-Yourself Home Encyclopaedia
William Collins, 1976

The Complete Homemaker
Marshall Cavendish, 1976

Decoration with Fabrics
David Hicks
Britwell Books, 1971

Design for Modern Living
Gerd Hatje and Peter Kaspar
Thames & Hudson, 1975

Fabrics for Interiors
Jack Lenor Larsen and Jeanne Weeks
Van Nostrand Reinhold, 1975

Flat Broke
Barbara Chandler
Pitman Publishing, 1976

Good Housekeeping
Do-It-Yourself Book
Albert Jackson and David Day
Ebury Press, 1977

The House Book
Terence Conran
Mitchell Beazley, 1974

How to Decorate without a Decorator
Mary Gilliatt
Thames & Hudson, 1977

Interior Decorating made Simple
Barty Phillips
Aldus Books, 1974

Interiors for Today
Franco Magnani
Studio Vista, 1975

Patchwork
Averil Colby
Batsford Books, 1976

The Pauper's Homemaking Book
Jocasta Innes
Penguin Books, 1976

Practical Guide to Colour and Design for the Home
Jill Blake
Publications for Companies, 1978

Reader's Digest Household Manual
Reader's Digest Association, 1977

Good Housekeeping Home Book
Ebury Press, 1978

For practical advice on planning and furnishing individual rooms – living rooms, kitchens, bathrooms, bedsitting rooms, children's rooms and workrooms – you should refer to the other Design Centre Books.

Acknowledgments

We are very grateful to the following firms who kindly supplied us with decorative materials, furniture and accessories for our three living room settings (see cover and pages 4 and 5):

ICI, who most generously gave us all the paint (Dulux and Vymura), wallpaper (Vymura), curtain and cushion fabrics (Vymura) and carpet tiles (Dulux);

Abstracta (chrome and glass units);

Beaver & Tapley (wall units);

Boyle & Son (Woolweave wallcovering);

E H Bradley Building Products (Bradstone fireplace);

Greenwood & Coope (Langford carpet);

Harrison Drape (curtain track);

Hodkin & Jones (fibrous plaster fireplace surround);

Hunter Douglas (Luxaflex curtain pole and blinds);

Nairn Floors (Nairnflex vinyl tiles);

Shelley Textiles (Tumbel Twist rugs);

Tablos (occasional table);

Thorn Lighting (light fittings);

Robert Whiting Designs (upholstered furniture).